PRAISE FOR
Personal & Authentic

"In *Personal & Authentic*, Tom Murray taps into some of the deepest emotions we all share and know are essential as educators and parents. He helps us to focus on the relationships that we develop with children and adults, the self-reflection that we learn quickly is so important, and the impact we make on our schools and communities. After you read this book, you will become a better teacher and leader. And if not, you might want to read it again!"

—*Salome Thomas-EL, award-winning principal, speaker, and author*

"One of the most helpful, heartfelt, and unassuming stories I've ever read. Thomas C. Murray sets a new standard for what it means to be *Personal & Authentic*. This is the book educators will be telling their friends, mentees, and future generations of educators about."

—*Brad Gustafson, national distinguished principal and best-selling author*

"As educators, we often are so busy doing the intricate, intentional work of good teaching that we don't allow ourselves time to stop and reflect on the larger impact of our profession. *Personal & Authentic* gives us this much-needed time while weaving in space for reflection, suggestions from fellow educators, as well as easy-to-implement practical tips for all educators. Teachers will finish this book feeling inspired and empowered to continue the important work we are called to do."

—*Luisa Palomo Hare, kindergarten teacher, 2012 Nebraska Teacher of the Year*

"In his inspirational book, Tom Murray helps educators make the connection between personal and authentic experiences through the power of storytelling. This philosophy sets the foundation for meeting the needs of students by building equitable opportunities for success. As Tom eloquently demonstrates in this book, in order for fundamental change to occur, one must remember it is all about fostering meaningful relationships first—everything else comes second!"

—*Basil Marin, high school assistant principal, Georgia*

"Wow! What an awesome source of inspiration, motivation, and hope for the future of our humans (students) and all those leaders in the education ecosystem that will have an impact on them. *Personal & Authentic* is a perfect description of this book, as Tom engages both the mind and the heart—making every word and interaction count. This book is for everyone! Tom's journey and lessons along the way will have you both in tears and laughing out loud. Give *Personal & Authentic* as a gift to yourself and share it widely! Thank you, Tom, for showing us the power of vulnerability and authenticity in this deeply personal connection to building a lifetime of impact."

—*David Miyashiro, superintendent, Cajon Valley Union School District, California*

"The story always wins. The most impactful learning has always been personal and authentic. Murray does a masterful job of weaving both the gripping story of educators and the opportunities for them to increase their impact on students. The text takes the reader on an emotional ride but also provides the challenge and resources to get better. The ideas jump off the page and will help anyone rediscover both the *why* and *how* to improve their space. This book is an essential piece of every educator's toolbox and one I know I'll go back to often."

—*Joe Sanfelippo*, PhD, superintendent, author, and speaker

"Murray has created yet another resource for teachers looking to make schools more impactful for students. *Personal & Authentic* not only demonstrates why our schools need to be built around what is best for each child but also gives the tools and strategies to get it done."

—*Josh Stumpenhorst*, high school librarian, 2012 Illinois Teacher of the Year

"This book had me crying, laughing, and feeling inspired to work with students and teachers. When we think about the work we do each and every day, it can connect on such a deeper level when it includes the personal and authentic pieces of the human experience. As Murray says, 'Every child in our schools is someone else's whole world.' We have the opportunity to provide unique opportunities to each and every student!"

—*A.J. Juliani*, director of learning and innovation, author, and founder of the PBL Academy

"Students yearn for a learning experience that resonates with them on many levels. The time is now to usher in the needed change in this area so that school means something to those it is designed to serve. Tom Murray takes you on an emotional roller coaster where you will see firsthand why a shift to more relevant techniques will benefit kids now and in the future."

—*Eric Sheninger*, NASSP digital principal and senior fellow, International Center for Leadership in Education

"Tom Murray takes you on a roller coaster of emotions throughout his book, *Personal & Authentic*. His heartfelt message of connection, empathy, and the need for equal opportunities for all students will leave you, regardless of your role in education, feeling inspired and wanting to do more for all kids. This book will touch the very depth of your core and remind you that every day is an opportunity to change the trajectory of a student's life. A must-read for all schools!"

—*Jimmy Casas*, educator, author, speaker, leadership coach

"What a privilege it was to read this book! As a fan of Tom Murray's work, I knew his newest endeavor would be great, but what I didn't expect was to find it chock-full of stories, social science, and surprises. Educators—at least those who want to 'move' people—should own this book. Finding a book for my teachers that can be easily learned from, regardless of their setting, grade level, or subject matter, is priceless . . . the only qualifier for reading is that that you have a heart and passion for kids."

—*Amber Teamann*, principal, author, speaker

"Tom Murray has found a way to weave heart-tugging stories, connected to research, and practical tips that can provide a profound impact on education today. *Personal & Authentic* will leave a lasting imprint on how you lead at school, home, and in life."

—*Jessica Cabeen*, *nationally distinguished principal, author, and speaker*

"The perfect title for a leader who 'practices what he preaches,' Tom Murray's latest book *Personal & Authentic: Designing Learning Experiences that Impact a Lifetime* captures what we are all looking for as educators: a powerful approach to achieving success at both the classroom and district level. The book serves as an exemplary overview for achieving both personalization and authenticity in our schools and classrooms."

—*Suzanne Lacey, EdD*, *superintendent, Talladega County Schools, Alabama*

"*Personal & Authentic* is a story from the heart. Tom Murray shares powerful stories from his teaching career as he conveys the importance of educating the whole child. I encourage anyone in the education field to read this book. The message resonates with teachers, leaders, and everyone involved in a school by inspiring everyone to get to know the kids, let them tell their story, and, above all else, show them you care."

—*Jerry Almendarez*, *superintendent, Colton Joint Unified School District, California*

"Tom Murray has poured his heart and soul into *Personal & Authentic*. This book is filled with compelling stories and examples that will inspire you to create learner-centered experiences that ensure students are equipped to not only succeed in school but lead meaningful lives. In a time when many educators are asked to do more than ever, this book serves as a powerful reminder about why our work matters and how we can prioritize the experiences that bring out the best in our students and each other."

—*Katie Martin*, *educator, author of* Learner-Centered Innovation

"As a follower of Tom's work for years, I have witnessed how his heart for children has touched so many of our colleagues. *Personal & Authentic* is no exception. Through the triangulation of personal stories, research, and practical tips from others in the field, this book is powerful, informative, and engaging. I highly recommend it!"

—*Sarah Thomas, PhD*, *regional technology coordinator, affiliate faculty, and founder of EduMatch®*

"*Personal & Authentic* is a true reflection of the title. Tom not only shares stories that share his core values and beliefs through the personal stories that he tells, but the tips he includes from other educators show a glimpse of their core values and beliefs as well. If you are looking for a read that cuts straight to the middle and touches the heart, but then leads to actionable results that will transform you as an educator and the relationships and experiences you encounter each day, *Personal & Authentic* is your go-to resource. This book will help you reflect, recharge, and refocus on the most important aspects of education—relationships and relevant learning experiences."

—*Sanée Bell, EdD*, *principal, speaker, author of* Be Excellent on Purpose: Intentional Strategies for Impactful Leadership

Personal & AUTHENTIC

DESIGNING LEARNING EXPERIENCES
THAT IMPACT A LIFETIME

THOMAS C. MURRAY

PERSONAL & AUTHENTIC

© 2019 by Thomas C. Murray

This book is available at special discounts when purchased in quantity for use as premiums, promotions, fundraisers, or for educational use. For inquiries and details, contact the publisher at books@impressbooks.org.

Published by IMPress, a division of Dave Burgess Consulting, Inc.
ImpressBooks.org
daveburgessconsulting.com

Editing, Interior, and Cover Design by My Writers' Connection

Library of Congress Control Number: 2019951888
Paperback ISBN: 978-1-948334-19-8
eBook ISBN: 978-1-948334-20-4

First Printing: October 2019

CONTENTS

THE WORK IS HARD, BUT OUR KIDS ARE WORTH IT.

FOREWORD

"Son, I love you, and I believe in you," were the words he said that I'll never forget. In my entire life, this was my very first encounter of a *personal* and *authentic* moment with a male who truly cared for and believed in me. Those words were spoken by Mr. DeMarco Mitchell, who, at twenty-three years old, was my eighth-grade math teacher and basketball coach.

I was born to a sixteen-year-old single mother, and we lived in a two-bedroom home on the eastside of Atlanta. It was located in one of the roughest places in America, and that home was where fourteen of us lived. This was a household and environment filled with drugs, gangs, and violence. As a child, one night each week, I'd have the opportunity to sleep in the bed. Most nights, I'd sleep on the floor. Each morning, I'd stand at the bus stop before school and shake out my bookbag to make sure no mice or rats had made their way into it during the night.

I didn't want to become a statistic. I wanted to break a generational curse on my family, one where nobody had ever been to college. Since I was seven years old, I wanted to play in the NFL so my mom and family would never have to miss another meal.

Growing up as I did, the most dangerous part of it all was that low expectations and failure was normal and acceptable. It was a way of life for those I lived with, many of whom are still in and out of prison, and those who lived in our part of the city. Life gave me every excuse not to succeed, but I was blessed to have had a teacher who refused to give up on me, even with my circumstances.

Every night, my cousin and I would go out to the street and race light pole to light pole wearing no shoes. I knew achieving my dreams meant that I had to put in the work, and I was determined to make it happen. I remember this one night, standing on the corner in my neighborhood surrounded by drug dealers, and that same teacher, the one who wouldn't stop believing in me, pulled up and said, "Inky, you're better than this." Although I wasn't engaging in any illegal activity, he knew the danger I was in—not only personally but also my dreams, goals, aspirations, beliefs, and potential—just by being present.

As my coach and mentor, he proceeded to speak to me as if we were in the midst of one of our basketball games. He looked me in the eyes and said, "Here's how we're going to beat this. I'm going to pick you up every morning before school and play you in a game of one-on-one basketball. Then we will study and learn Proverbs until you graduate high school." To be honest, I thought our game plan would last probably a year, maybe less. But I was wrong. My teacher showed up, picked me up for school, day after day, and poured into me. He did whatever it took to support me. He believed in me.

I'll never forget the day the principal approached him in our gymnasium and said, "I heard you've been talking about the Proverbs with Inky." Mr. Mitchell said, "Yes, sir, I have." The principal reminded him of the separation of church and state and said that he could lose his job if it continued. Mr. Mitchell replied, saying he would just have to get fired then because *my life was worth it*. I remember walking home from school that day thinking that if my teacher was willing to put the way he provides for his wife and kids on the line for me, I had to make him proud, give him my best, and not let him down.

Needless to say, he didn't get fired. He did whatever was needed to help me. To this day, Mr. DeMarco Mitchell is still my mentor. It's been nine years since he walked my wife down the aisle at our wedding. He will always be the man in my eyes who showed he cared more about me than he did about my grades, test scores, and sports. He wanted me to know and understand what *personal* and *authentic* love and connection looks and feels like. He would often tell me, "My press in life is to VALUE you more than I value what I believe about you." As a teacher, his impact on my life, and the lives of others, has now been passed on to the next generation.

I'm a firm believer that things don't happen to you. They happen *for* you. The funny thing about my injury was that my life found new meaning and new purpose. Instead of the injury serving as a curse, it has served as a blessing. It's an opportunity. You see, my arm may be paralyzed, but my heart isn't. My mind isn't. My attitude isn't. The same arm the doctor told me I would never use again because of paralysis, I now use *every day* of my life. I believe you are not defined by your circumstances or your situation. You are defined by your decisions and your choices. Every day I make a decision to make my life count. Every day I'm going to work to inspire someone. Every day I'm going to work to encourage someone.

As an educator, *you* get to do the same.

Much like Mr. DeMarco Mitchell, Tom is someone who is passionate about people and education. He is a friend whom I admire and respect. I'll never forget the first time I saw him speak to a school district and the way in which he thanked the school bus drivers, cafeteria workers, and custodial staff and how it pierced my heart. His love for teachers, administrators, support staff, and kids is something that is very *personal* for him. If I had to use one word to describe him, it would be *authentic*. He values people and understands the lifelong impact each person can have in whatever role they serve. He understands how, as educators, your fingerprints remain on the lives of others for generations to come.

This book, *Personal & Authentic: Designing Learning Experiences that Impact a Lifetime*, is going to serve as a source of encouragement to people all over the world, and I'm excited to see it manifest!

With much love and respect,

Inky Johnson
@InkyJohnson
Inkyjohnson.com
ESPN Story Emmy Nominated

DEDICATION

Professionally, this book is dedicated to the countless teachers who pour their lives into other people's children every day. You dedicate your work to supporting those who desperately need you. May your fingerprints of impact be on the lives of those you serve for generations to come.

Personally, this book is dedicated to my parents, Tom and Cherie Murray. God couldn't have given me more when he allowed me to call you Mom and Dad. You've sacrificed so much to help propel me forward, and for that, I'll be eternally grateful. You are models of perseverance, resilience, overcoming life's challenges, living life with love and humility, and ultimately, what it means to be *personal* and *authentic*. Love you both so much, and I'm honored to call you my parents.

via Merriam-Webster:

PERSONAL (adjective)
per·son·al | \ 'pərs-nəl, 'pər-sə-nəl\
: of, relating to, or affecting a particular person

AUTHENTIC (adjective)
au·then·tic | \ ə-'then-tik, ȯ-\
: true to one's own personality, spirit, or character

THE
Personal
&AUTHENTIC
FRAMEWORK

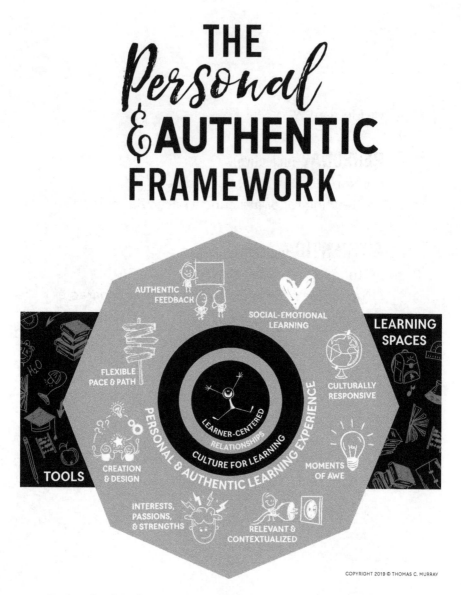

To download the framework, visit **thomascmurray.com/AuthenticEDU**.

The words *personal* and *authentic* describe much of the work we do as educators. Whether describing a learner-centered experience, our relationships with students and colleagues, the culture of our schools and classrooms, or the legacies we leave, the syntax of *personal* and *authentic* can mean different things under different constructs, yet often go hand in hand. This book explores many ways in which these ideas interconnect and how being *personal* and *authentic* in our work will positively impact those we serve. When fused together, this Personal & Authentic Framework can help guide our work and empower us to leave impactful, long-lasting legacies. Here's a quick overview of what you can expect from this book:

In Chapter 1, you'll read part of my story and discover how I formed my personal educational lens. You'll clearly see how I came to understand what this work is about, how being *personal* and *authentic* helps to define our relationships with those we serve, and how it must remain core to all that we do as educators. You'll immediately see why the learner is at the center of this framework and how relationships surround it.

Chapter 2 guides you in understanding how *personal* and *authentic* can help define the culture for learning that our students need to thrive. Beginning with a focus on you as the reader, I hope this chapter will challenge your leadership mindset and help you make every interaction matter by building trust and taking calculated risks along the way. In the framework, this culture for learning reinforces the relationships and remains at the center of the student experience.

In Chapter 3, we'll explore the *personal* and *authentic* stories hidden within each person to make sure that when we see our students, we not only see faces but hearts as well. Starting with why, we'll seek out ways to prioritize each child's story to find the unique beauty inside.

In Chapters 4 and Chapter 5, we'll build on the relationships and culture for learning aspects of the framework to envision and design *personal* and *authentic* learning experiences for our students. From creating the vision and being intentional with our first impressions to exploring many of the ways in which the student learning experience can be *personal* and *authentic*, these two chapters outline practical ways to support each student as a valued individual on a unique journey.

Chapter 6 helps us rethink the use of tools and spaces and ultimately refocus on how to effectively leverage them as part of a *personal* and *authentic* experience. Seen as framework supports, these facets can either amplify or hinder the student experience. As such, we'll explore issues surrounding equity, first by recognizing the gaps in opportunity and access that still exist for marginalized groups, and second by identifying ways to tackle these vital issues head-on in our classrooms and schools.

In Chapter 7, we'll bring it all together so we can maximize our *personal* and *authentic* legacy as educators. It is only through perseverance and resilience and by developing a fail-forward mindset through adversity that we can make it happen.

Throughout this book, you'll learn from dozens of educators as they share their tips to **"Make It Stick,"** giving you practical ways to maximize *personal* and *authentic* learning in your classroom or school. I wrote the **"Stop & Reflect"** questions specifically to make you pause and reflect on your own practice, as we know that reflection is a key component of growth and the start of any change in practice. You'll also have the opportunity to see *personal* and *authentic* experiences **"In Practice"** through the supplemental vignettes, which were written by some of today's leading educators, who have shared their stories of making their student experiences both *personal* and *authentic*. Most sections conclude with ways you can **"Try This."** Written to support your work, whether in leading a classroom or a school, these examples offer practical and tangible ideas that you can implement immediately. Finally, you'll have the opportunity to take **"A Closer Look"** at some behind-the-scenes video footage as well as many tools and resources that correlate with the ideas found inside each chapter.

Throughout these pages, as you reflect upon the work you do each day, I encourage you to share your thoughts using the hashtag **#AuthenticEDU**. Together, let's amplify the many amazing things happening in classrooms and schools each day while continuing to take steps forward on our own unique journeys.

chapter 1

RELATIONSHIPS: THE FOUNDATION OF PERSONAL & AUTHENTIC LEARNING

EVERY KID IS ONE CARING ADULT AWAY
FROM BEING A SUCCESS STORY.

—JOSH SHIPP

———

*I*s it possible to recognize a life-changing moment as it's happening? Or does the significance of those moments only become visible after the fact?

A life-changing moment happens in a blink. It's that moment where faith overcomes fear. It's the first step toward a new reality, a step that permanently alters your dreams and changes the way you think about your life—forever.

In my own life, I didn't see that moment for what it was until it had put me on a course that changed who I was and how I viewed my purpose—and yours—as an educator. The spark of a single piece of advice created opportunities for many moments—moments that were *personal* and *authentic*, and yes, life changing.

I was twenty-one years old and fresh out of college in my first year of teaching, and I thought I had a clue as to what I was getting myself into. I had always wanted to work with kids, and finally, I was getting my opportunity to do so as a brand-new fourth-grade teacher.

I spent countless hours that summer setting up my first classroom. Then, ripe with anticipation, the day finally came. My first opportunity. My very own students.

Mark Wieder, my mentor and a veteran teacher, taught across the hall in room 303. He had twenty-six years of teaching experience and was the heart and soul of our school. He was brilliant. He was funny. His kids excelled. He was exactly the kind of teacher I wanted to become. He was the kind of teacher every kid wanted.

How do I know?

On my very first day teaching, it seemed as if every student walked into my classroom hanging his or her head and saying, "I really wish I had Mr. Wieder this year."

Yes, really. And I couldn't blame them.

From the moment I met Mark, I understood why. He was passionate. He was fun. His love for people and for learning radiated in all that he did.

Just before my first day began, Mark and I stood in the hallway and talked for a few minutes, and I can remember my excitement to this day. It about paralleled the nerves I felt at the time. Just before the bell rang, Mark put his arm around my shoulders, looked at me, and said, "Tom, as your mentor, if there's one thing I can teach you, it's that this work is about loving and caring about kids. Everything else, and I mean everything else, is secondary to that. It's all about relationships. Tom, if you keep that core to all you do, you'll have amazing success in your career. If you lose sight of that, as your mentor, I'll give you two options: one, get out and go do something different, or two, refocus on it. The kids who are about to walk down this hallway need you. For some, you may be all that they have this year. Don't you ever forget that. Relationships first, everything else comes second."

The bell rang, and my first set of students walked down the hallway, ready for their first day of fourth grade. Little did I know, at that moment, what would happen over the course of the school year would fundamentally change who I was as an educator and who I was as a person. I'd learn more in that year about people, loving others, and what teaching was truly about than I had in any course, in any student-teaching experience, or in any previous life experience. My first school year would challenge me to my core and alter my mindset.

My first class of students was challenging. As much as I enjoyed working with them, they were a difficult group. Similar to previous years, many of them struggled with their behavior; albeit being brand new, I'm sure I also struggled as a teacher because I had so much to learn.

From across the hall, I'd watch Mark. His students laughed often, as did he. In the morning, kids would *run* to him. It seemed that every afternoon when the bell rang, people would come back to visit. Decades later, I still remember one particular Friday afternoon vividly.

A young couple, holding a baby, walked down the hallway toward Mark's room. I glanced at them, assuming they were the parents of one of his students, but I'd soon learn that they weren't.

"Mr. Wieder," the man said as he waved from the back of Mark's room. "I'm Sam. I was in your class twenty years ago. Do you remember me?"

Immediately, Mark responded, "Sam! Of course I do. Come on in."

Sam looked at his wife, smiled, and said, "Honey, this is the teacher I've always told you about, Mr. Wieder. That's him!" I watched in awe as Mark walked to the back of the room, gave Sam a huge hug, and then introduced himself to Sam's bride.

Sam went on, "Mr. Wieder, this is our baby girl. She's five months old now. We're here visiting my parents for the weekend, so I wanted her to meet my favorite teacher."

I was twenty-one years old. This man had been Mark's student the year after I was born, and Mark remembered Sam and his class after two decades. I watched in awe. Would that ever be me? Would students remember me and my classroom as they did his years later? Would students want to come back and visit me? Would I leave that type of legacy? Would I be the kind of teacher they'd tell their children about decades later?

As those first few weeks went on, I watched Mark lead. When he'd walk into the faculty room, people would smile. He made people laugh. Never once did I hear Mark complain. He brought his best every single day—and it showed. Mark practiced what he preached to his students. His students loved him for it and so did the team around him.

Meanwhile, across the hall, I was simply trying to survive. Like any new teacher, I found just keeping my head above water was a challenge. I wasn't concerned about long-term planning. I was more concerned about being ready for tomorrow (and sometimes just making it through the day). My students had a tremendous set of needs, and each day seemed to bring a different challenge. I was inexperienced, and I'm sure it really showed on more than one occasion.

I finally lost it in October of that first year. Having felt like I had exhausted every option and feeling deep down that I was failing, I exploded in the faculty room one day during lunch.

After a frustrating morning, I walked in, huffing and puffing, and threw myself into a chair, slamming my hand on the faculty room lunch table.

"He's not getting it!" I blurted out. "He's not changing. I call home almost every day. I hardly ever hear back. He's disrespectful. He doesn't listen. He does what he wants. I can't take it anymore. I hold him in for recess almost every day. The mom never even calls me back. I can't deal with this kid any more!"

On the verge of tears, I stood up and stormed out of the faculty room, huffed all the way back to my classroom, and let the door close behind me.

I didn't realize it at the time, but Mark had left his lunch on the table and followed me back down the hall to my classroom. Then my mentor opened my classroom door and closed it behind him.

Mark walked toward me, looked me straight in the eye, and said, "Tom, as your mentor, don't you ever, ever do that again. You want to get through to him? You need to love him. You need to care for him. You need to show him, every day, how much he matters. Tom, when he knows how much he matters, maybe then he'll start to show you that he cares."

"Tom, what did I tell you before that first day?" Mark asked. Without waiting for me to respond, he continued, "This work is all about relationships. This work is about loving and caring about kids. Without it, you have nothing. And right now, with this student, it looks like you have nothing. Instead of holding him in for recess, what if you asked him to have lunch to get to know him? Instead of yelling at him, what if you encouraged him the moment you saw something positive? Instead of calling home for being in trouble, what if you called home for something great? When do you think he last heard a compliment? When's the last time you think mom received a positive call home? If you want to get through to him, Tom, maybe it's you who needs to change."

Humility set in instantly. It was the lowest moment of my young career and, ultimately, one of the most humbling moments I have ever had as an educator. Tears streamed down my face as we stood together in my classroom that October afternoon. After some necessary (and deserved) harsh words, Mark stepped toward me, and this amazing teacher of twenty-six years leaned in and gave me a hug.

I realized at that moment that he had become emotional too. He truly cared for me. He desperately wanted me to succeed.

Mark then whispered softly, "You can do this, Tom. I believe in you."

He was spot on. *I* needed to change. It was *my heart* that had hardened.

In that moment, faith overcame fear. In that moment, empathy overcame my hard heart. In that moment, I realized relationships really were the foundation of our work as educators.

Later on that year, I'd learn that the child I struggled with had been the victim of one of the worst abuse cases I'd ever see in my entire career. *That* was the reason he acted the way that he did. When I started to take the time to see his heart and understand his story, I was no longer blinded by my own shaded lens. Just getting to school in the morning was an accomplishment for this boy. I had been so focused on myself that I couldn't see him. I had been so focused on my needs, so insistent that he conform to *my* rules and *my* ways of doing things, that I had completely missed looking at his heart and what it was that he really needed.

Mark was right. I will forever be grateful that I had a colleague, a true mentor, who called me out face-to-face and set me straight. He didn't gossip about my shortfalls in the faculty room. He coached me and challenged me when needed. He openly shared his experience, and through his example, I learned it was okay—even courageous—to ask for help. His mentorship ultimately changed the course of my career. And it was exponentially compounded by what happened next.

As the months went on, my respect for Mark grew. I watched as he asked our principal if he could take the first few minutes of a faculty meeting to lead a fun activity for the team. I watched him dress up for assemblies to make kids laugh. I watched as he created the type of classroom where kids *wanted to be*. He had high expectations for and loved every one of his students—and they thrived.

I no longer wondered why every fourth grader wanted Mr. Wieder as their teacher. Mark's students felt loved in his classroom. He challenged them and made them believe they could rise to meet his challenge. Mark impacted hundreds of students over the years. He made the learning experience *personal* and *authentic* for them. The relationships Mark had with his students and the way he fostered an inclusive culture made them feel like they belonged and could change the world. His relationships were the foundation of the success that occurred in that classroom.

Mark attracted people to him, students and staff alike. It wasn't his step on the pay scale, the bulletin boards that he hung, or how pretty his handouts were. He was a *personal* and *authentic* person. He treated others well, and he focused on relationships and loving others in everything he did.

Over the next few months, learning from Mark and other experienced colleagues, I began to change my practice. I found that as I changed my own mindset, my students responded—just as Mark had said they would. The experience of a veteran teacher is invaluable, and Mark guided me as only a true mentor could. My heart softened. When I changed my mindset from *what* I taught to *who* I taught, the real work came into focus. I began to understand the immense connection between *personal* and *authentic* relationships, classroom culture, and student learning outcomes.

As my attitude improved, so did my students' behavior.
As my love for them grew, so did their respect and concern for me.
As my heart opened, their lives could finally be poured into.
As a team, working through things together, we began to win.

Teachers are some of the only people on the planet who go to bed worrying about other people's children. Early on, I'd go to bed and stare at the ceiling with frustration from the day. Months later, after many lessons learned, I still lost a tremendous amount of sleep but for entirely different reasons. I'd gained immense empathy for all my students because I had a better understanding of what was on their plates, all they dealt with at home, and all the things I took for granted in life, for which their little hearts longed.

The months went on, and things improved. I received encouragement from other teachers, as well as guidance and support, and my confidence increased. I finally felt like maybe, just maybe, I could do this teaching thing.

WHEN I CHANGED MY MINDSET FROM *WHAT* I TAUGHT TO *WHO* I TAUGHT, THE REAL WORK CAME INTO FOCUS.

I'd soon learn that the next few months would be some of the most difficult that I would ever encounter. My core would be shaken. My confidence rattled. My heart broken. I would question over and over again if I had the courage to be a teacher. I often wondered if I had a strong enough heart to work with kids.

It was the Wednesday before spring break. Due to the upcoming break, students were dismissed early that afternoon. The previous night, Mark and his wife Rae Ann had picked up the brand-new fourteen-foot camper they had just purchased. He had such excitement in his voice as he showed me the pictures from the brochure and told me all about it that day.

"Check this part out, Tom. We can put the grill back here. The bedroom is back here," he'd said.

After school that day, Mark was heading home to pick up his wife to go and watch their son, Mark Jr., play tennis at his college in Maryland. They were going to get to use their beautiful new camper for the first time, and I was excited for them. As we stood in the hallway that afternoon and wished each other a great, long weekend, I waved and said, "Have a great time, Mark! Enjoy the new camper! Have a safe trip. I'll see you on Tuesday!"

I didn't realize it until later that everything changed in that moment because those would be my last words to Mark. I didn't know that moment would be our last. I didn't know that goodbye would be my final goodbye to my mentor.

If only I could have said "thank you" one more time.

The following morning, I walked outside to retrieve the local newspaper from the box at the end of my driveway. I looked down at the front-page headline: "Couple from Macungie Killed in Fiery Accident on Turnpike."

Image Credit: *The Morning Call*, reprinted with permission

I began to read the front-page news.

A sport utility vehicle pulling a trailer ran out of control and skidded off the Northeast Extension of the Pennsylvania Turnpike south of the Quakertown interchange, catching fire and killing a Macungie couple Wednesday afternoon. Mark Alton Wieder, 48, and Rae Ann Wieder, 50, both of 30 S. Sycamore St., were killed, state police at King of Prussia said.

> ## Make It Stick
>
> "Conduct 'working lunches' with small groups of students. Create, build, innovate, and publish together."
> "Schedule time to check in with students on their turf after discipline-type conversations. Relationships are built over time."
>
> —Brad Gustafson, EdD, elementary school principal, Minnesota

Only those who have experienced sudden tragedy with loved ones can understand the fear, the anger, the disbelief, and the raw emotion that ensues in moments like these.

Wieder's vehicle, which was pulling the fourteen-foot camper trailer, went off the road and struck the guardrail with the right front bumper, police said. The SUV separated from the trailer, became airborne, and slid down an embankment. It spun clockwise before striking a tree on the driver's side, police said.

The SUV fell about thirty feet from the highway to Kumry Road, said Bucks County Coroner Joseph Campbell. The road was slick from a steady rain that fell throughout the day. Campbell said gasoline leaking from the vehicle caught fire and gutted the vehicle with the driver and passenger trapped inside.

"The fire was pretty extensive," Campbell said. "It was a pretty violent accident." Campbell said Mark Wieder died of smoke inhalation, burns, and trauma, and his wife died of burn and smoke inhalation. Firefighters arrived on the scene to find the car in flames, fire officials said.[1]

In that moment, my mentor—an amazing husband, dad of two, family man, and one of the best teachers that has ever walked this earth—and his loving wife were gone. Like so many others, heartbroken doesn't begin to describe the grief that those who knew the couple felt.

That afternoon, many of my colleagues came together at school to mourn the loss of our friend. We shared stories of the man he was as our hearts were heavy. We cried together. We loved on one another, holding each other's hearts in our hands.

I've come to realize that you never really know when that moment will be. You never really know when it will happen. You only know once that moment has passed, and reality has become a memory.

The last smile.

The last high five.

The last hug.

The last goodbye.

Mark's life was cut way too short. Yet during his forty-eight years, he fully lived. He lived every day to the fullest. Mark had more joy and found more happiness through his relationships in forty-eight years than many feel in a lifetime. He epitomized the true impact of a teacher.

The following Saturday, over 4,000 people paid their respects to Mark and Rae Ann Wieder. Lines circled the church in Macungie, Pennsylvania, and people waited for hours to say their goodbye to two people they respected and loved so much.

I'm not sure if Mark ever grasped the actual impact he had as a teacher, the legacy he built, or the lives he helped change course, including mine. Sometimes I wonder if we'll ever really know how long our fingerprints, as educators, will last on those we have the privilege to serve. Mark's fingerprints will be seen on the lives of others for generations.

THE IMPACT OF A TEACHER

Never say that you are *just* a teacher. You have *just* the right opportunity, every day, to change the lives of kids—just like my mentor Mark Wieder did, for over two-and-a-half decades.

Mark's passing helped me understand that the quality of our relationships dictates our personal happiness. Ultimately, these relationships solidify and authenticate our successes. For Mark, these relationships were plentiful. They were personal in nature. They were authentic in experience. They were the foundation of all he did, both at home and at school. They are his legacy.

In our schools and classrooms, we need to ensure that students are not experience rich and relationship poor. It is in the quality of your relationships where your legacy as an educator will live.

I've come to learn that the more *personal* and *authentic* we are, the greater our impact will be. As educators, our effectiveness is based on the quality of our relationships. These relationships are the foundation of our work, the center of our why.

NEVER SAY THAT YOU ARE *JUST* A TEACHER. YOU HAVE *JUST* THE RIGHT OPPORTUNITY, EVERY DAY, TO CHANGE THE LIVES OF KIDS.

As an educator, your fingerprints remain on the lives of those you serve. The greater your impact, the more profound and long-lasting the prints will be. Your daily work alters the course of history as you mold and shape the lives of others and that of future generations. Your fingerprints and legacy change the course of humanity. But you determine how it will change through the choices you make and the relationships you build.

Another month passed, and our school family was still grieving. All who have experienced the loss of a loved one know how difficult moving forward can be. We didn't hide our grief. We worked together to face our new reality, and it reflected in our work.

For an authentic writing experience, I asked the kids to write a short essay answering the following prompt:

"Write a descriptive paragraph about someone that you admire. Make sure to include as many reasons as you can that tell why you admire that person. Make sure to include things you have seen the person do that have inspired you."

Selfishly for me, it was an opportunity to write about Mark. It was an opportunity to write down the many ways his life touched mine. It was an opportunity for me to be vulnerable in front of my students. It was an opportunity for me to show humility. It was an opportunity to continue to grieve. It was an opportunity for me to finally take a step forward.

I shared how, as a new teacher, I admired Mark Wieder for who he was. I admired him for his integrity and how his love for others radiated in everything he did. I admired the teacher he was and how his kids loved being in his class. I also shared how I admired Mark for having the courage to call me out when I was wrong and to help me become a better teacher. For me, Mark defined the true meaning of a teacher, as he was far more than a content deliverer—he was a life changer.

That week, I shared my writing with my students and used it as a model for their work. I shed many tears throughout the writing process and was amazed at my students' responses to my vulnerability as I shared my heart with them. Our team had transformed from a group of students previously known for behavioral issues to a team of kids who would be bound together forever by tragedy.

Make It Stick

"Make time each day to connect with every child. We are all pressed for time, but that connection can make a lifelong impact. Remember their hobbies, activities, siblings, and bring them up to show genuine interest in the people around you."

"Enjoy the time that you spend with your students. Smile, laugh, and show them who you really are."

—Lee Moyer, elementary school teacher, Pennsylvania

The following Monday, the students finished and handed in their essays. I still remember many of them being unable to stop talking about the person they wrote about because of the impact that person had on them. They had excitement in their voices and love in their eyes. They were proud.

That night I read the essays with joy. Faith wrote about her mom, Bryan wrote about his favorite baseball player, and Alyssa wrote about her gymnastics coach. And then I read what Cody had written.

Cody wasn't your typical student. He was a student I knew I needed to find ways to reach. He was one of the students I knew needed extra love. He was also one of the students that Mark helped me learn to understand. After Mark pushed me to really get to know my kids, I began eating lunch with students one-on-one each day to get to know them as people rather than just as learners.

Cody was one of those students who marched to his own drum. During recess, most times, he'd wander the playground on his own. He'd often come to school with mismatched clothes or missing his homework. It was during our first lunch together the previous November that my heart began to connect to his. When I asked Cody what his biggest goals were that year, he smiled faintly and said he "was hoping to make a friend that year." I remember holding back tears the moment I internalized it. I remember feeling awful that it had taken me until November to know that about him. We had spent so much time together in the classroom, yet I hardly knew his heart. I remember promising myself in that moment that I would do whatever it took to help him. Before I could really teach him, I had to try to understand him.

Over the following months, Cody and I ate lunch together regularly. As Mark had suggested, I'd play soccer with him at recess, and other students would join in. I learned of his love for science and video games. I discovered his fun-loving, quirky personality. The more I got to know Cody, the more he knew I cared for him. His attendance and grades began to improve. He began to display some confidence, and his smile began to show more frequently. The day he came in telling me about his two best friends in the class, he wore one of the biggest smiles I'd ever see on him.

After a few moments of reflection, I read Cody's essay. He had written about me.

> I admire Mr. Murray because he also helps me with things that I need help on. He believes I can do it. He thinks I am a good student, he really likes me and he knows I can get good grades. I like him very much for believing I can do well and to be a better student. I try to work hard to make him smile. I like Mr. Murray very much. So I am going be a better Student for him.

Tears flowed from the moment I saw my name on his paper following the word *admire*. For the first time, I felt that even as a brand-new teacher, with so much to learn, I could have an impact on the lives of others. I finally had that feeling, one that Mark probably had countless times over his career.

I spent the rest of that evening feeling proud of my kids. They shared their hearts with me through their writing and articulated why they admired others with such detail.

Students were off the following day, as it was a teacher in-service day. After spending the majority of the morning with the other fourth-grade teachers in the district and then going out to lunch with my team, we returned for the afternoon sessions. Soon into that afternoon session, a voice said over the loudspeaker, "Tom Murray, if you're in the building, please come to the office."

My colleagues looked at me, perplexed. I had a sinking feeling; something just didn't feel right. I grabbed my bag, packed up my stuff, and stepped out into the hallway. One of the district administrators, Karen Beerer, was walking toward me. I will never forget what she said to me: "Tom, it's not your family, but something's happened." We walked downstairs to the main office. She couldn't bring herself to say much else.

We entered the high school principal's office and someone closed the door behind us. As I sat in the chair they had pulled out for me, I looked around the room and saw the superintendent, the two assistant superintendents, and my school principal, Bill Gretzula, who had tears in his eyes. Bill had been a rock of courage and support for me since Mark's loss. He said, "Tom, this morning something terrible happened."

I remember feeling like I wasn't strong enough to hear what he was about to say. I can remember bracing myself for the worst.

Bill continued, "This morning, while at home, Cody passed away."

My tears fell like rain and wouldn't stop. What did stop, however, was my world at that moment.

Bill went on to share additional details of what they knew about how the death occurred. "I'm so sorry, Tom. I know how close you were with him."

Cody was ten.

The flashbacks began immediately. I remembered spending lunch with him, kicking the ball with him at recess, and his beautiful smile. Closing my eyes, I could hear his laugh from the day before. I had flashbacks of the times he mistakenly called me "Dad." I recalled the ten-year-old boy in my class that I'd grown to have a *personal* and *authentic* relationship with, a student that I had loved.

I never had the chance to return Cody's essay to him. I was never able to share with him how much his words and encouragement meant to me.

If I'd only had one more chance. If I'd only had one more opportunity.

Police ruled Cody's death due to "accidental causes." To this day, I hope and pray that was the case. For a child who was dealt a very tough set of cards in life and for all he shared, I'll forever wish I did more for him.

As a brand-new teacher who was already struggling emotionally due to the loss of my mentor and friend, I went from heartache to feeling like I couldn't go on. I can honestly say that I didn't believe I had the strength or the courage it takes to be a teacher.

The following Saturday, I went to another funeral—my second in five weeks. This time, it wasn't for a well-known teacher whose life was celebrated by thousands and thousands of people. This time, it was a small service with a handful of family members, a few neighbors, and a few classmates with their parents, who exhibited far more courage than I could have dreamed, to pay respects to their fourth-grade friend.

Saying goodbye to Cody that final time was another defining moment for me as an educator. As I stood there saying goodbye, tears for this boy I had grown to love streaming down my face, I promised myself that no child would ever come through my doors without knowing they were cared for and loved. No child would ever walk through my classroom door without being told, and more importantly shown, that I'd do whatever it took to show them how much they mattered.

Mark's relationships with others defined who he was and helped me see who I wanted and needed to be. Cody's relationship with me helped define who I was and who I needed to be—for him and for every child who walked through my classroom door.

THE BEST THING THAT WE CAN GIVE KIDS THIS SCHOOL YEAR IS NOT A NEW CURRICULUM OR TECHNOLOGY; IT'S AN EMPATHETIC HEART THAT SEES AND HEARS THEIRS.

As we begin our journey to make learning *personal* and *authentic*, know that the work starts with us. If we want to leave a lasting legacy, as every educator does, the work begins in us. The best thing that we can give kids this school year is not a new curriculum or technology; it's an empathetic heart that sees and hears theirs. The foundation of creating learner-centered, personal, and authentic experiences is, and always will be, relationships.

It is *our* mindset. *Our* lens. *Our* way of thinking. *Our* relationships. That's where learning that is *personal* and *authentic* begins. Education begins and ends with people, and we must own our roles in this process. When we become more concerned about what we teach than who we teach, we have lost the purpose of the work. We must look deep inside ourselves and discover who we are before we can impact anything outside ourselves and, ultimately, who our students will become.

We must love our kids more than we love our pasts. We must love our kids more than we love our habits. We must love our kids more than we love our own egos. We must love our kids enough to change ourselves when needed.

The work is hard. The work is stressful. The work is emotional. But our kids are worth it.

Together, we can do this.

Stop & REFLECT

How would you design a student learning experience if the quality of the relationship was at the core? What *personal* and *authentic* experiences have impacted you as an educator? Share them on social media, using the hashtag #AuthenticEDU.

WHEN WE BECOME MORE CONCERNED ABOUT *WHAT* WE TEACH THAN WHO WE TEACH, WE HAVE LOST THE PURPOSE OF THE WORK.

Try This

> Ask the previous year's teacher, or a family member if necessary, the proper pronunciation of the child's name and what she prefers to be called.

> Be vulnerable and authentic with students and don't be afraid to be transparent about your own struggles and challenges. Such a perception makes you approachable and relatable.

> Begin the day with three Post-it notes on your desk. Over the course of the day, write a brief note to three different students, highlighting something you appreciate, recognize, or that makes you proud. After students have left for the day, place the three notes in a creative place where the student will find it the next day, such as inside a locker, on the textbook page he will open to next, or in a folder inside her desk.

> Designate a classroom greeter who is responsible to greet each student at the door each morning or before the class period every day for a week. Students enter with their choice of a handshake, high-five, or fist bump, and a hello by name.

> Early in the day (for elementary students) or at the beginning of the class period (for secondary students), provide a "one-minute reflection" opportunity. Students can ask a question about the previous day's content, reflect on what they just learned, or share something currently on their hearts with the teacher. Handing in the reflection can be optional or completed through a digital tool such as Google Forms. This allows every student to provide confidential feedback in only a few minutes.

> Don't simply tell students that you care; show them that you do. Empty words become meaningless, whereas modeling through your actions enables *personal* and *authentic* connections.

A CLOSER LOOK

For a deeper dive into Chapter 1 as well as free tools, resources, and study guide questions, visit **thomascmurray.com/AuthenticEDU1**.

Make It Stick

"Don't be afraid to push the lesson aside and just talk to your students. It's okay to make time for meaningful conversations. Every kid, every day."

"Use your own lens to view your students. Begin the school year giving each student a clean slate and see the student rather than previous behaviors."

—Rachelle Dene Poth, high school teacher, Pennsylvania

chapter 2

CREATING A CULTURE FOR LEARNING

WE MAY NOT GET THE CHANCE TO CHOOSE WHICH KIDS OR
FAMILIES TO SERVE, BUT WE DO GET TO DECIDE WHAT KIND
OF CLIMATE WE WANT TO SERVE THEM IN.

—JIMMY CASAS

For learning to be *personal* and *authentic*, a dynamic learning culture must exist. Developing such a culture, whether as a teacher in a classroom, a principal in a building, or a superintendent of a district, becomes possible when four core pillars are solidified. It is on these pillars where such a culture can be built. Ultimately, it is within this culture where a shift in the learning experience for kids becomes possible.

The four pillars to create a dynamic learning culture:

1. Leadership
2. Interactions
3. Trust
4. Risk-taking

For learning to be *personal* and *authentic*, these pillars must be intentionally reinforced and done so regularly. A culture for learning is bound in the strength of these pillars.

Stop & REFLECT

Which of these pillars is strongest in your classroom or school? Which needs to be solidified the most?

LEADERSHIP STARTS WITH YOU

"What you do has far greater impact than what you say."
—STEPHEN COVEY

I've had the privilege of working for some fantastic leaders over the years. Those leaders had courage. They had articulate, kid-centered visions. They valued people first and helped foster cultures of risk-taking and innovation. Those leaders modeled the way, led by example, and saw kids as far more than data points and test scores. They were willing to challenge the status quo and do whatever it took for the students they served. They understood that to be effective, they had to lead by being *personal* and *authentic*.

Working with educators in the United States and throughout the world gives me great hope. Spending time with educators every week affords me the insight as to the vast array of work that's being done to support our students. Many incredible things happen in classrooms every day.

I've worked with amazing leaders in states like Mississippi where 100 percent of the students where I served lived below the poverty line. In places like this, I've met dynamic, passionate, and talented educators who serve brilliant, determined, hard-working, and courageous kids.

I've also spent time on the other end of the financial spectrum, in some of our country's wealthiest suburbs, where outfitting the newest virtual reality and STEM lab with the latest technology and spending tens of thousands of dollars on such products each year is more than feasible. In places like this, I've also met dynamic, passionate, and talented educators who serve brilliant, determined, hard-working, and courageous kids.

If I'm fully transparent in these thoughts, the converse is also true. I've worked with leaders in some of the most impoverished areas and leaders in some of the wealthiest areas whose leadership I'd struggle to place my own children under. These interactions have been limited, as the vast amount of school and district leaders I work with are people-loving, kid-centered, dynamic, and talented individuals who pour their hearts into other people's children each day.

With the vast experiences mentioned above, from urban to rural, from large to small, and from poor to wealthy, incredible educators can be found in every demographic.

What I've come to know is . . .

. . . a school's budget doesn't make a great leader.

. . . a school's location doesn't make a great leader.

. . . a school's size doesn't make a great leader.

. . . a person's title doesn't make a great leader.

In *Learning Transformed: 8 Keys to Designing Tomorrow's Schools, Today*, Eric Sheninger and I address this issue as we contrast "Leaders by Title" (LBTs) with "Leaders by Action" (LBAs):

In our opinion, the best leaders have one thing in common: they do, as opposed to just talk. Leadership is about action, not position or chatter. Some of the best leaders we have seen during our years in education have never held any sort of administrative title. They had the tenacity to act on a bold vision for change to improve learning for kids and the overall school culture. These people are often overlooked and may not be considered "school leaders" because they don't possess the necessary title or degree that is used to describe a leader in the traditional sense. Nevertheless, the effect these leaders can have on an organization is much greater than an LBT. We need more leaders by action (LBA). Make no mistake about the fact that you are surrounded by these people each day. They are teachers, students, parents, support staff members, and administrators who have taken action to initiate meaningful change in their classrooms or schools. These leaders don't just talk the talk; they also walk the walk. They lead by example in what might be the most effective way possible: by modeling. They don't expect others to do what they aren't willing to do. It doesn't take a title or a new position for these leaders to be agents of change. LBAs drive sustainable change and make the transformation of learning possible.

Never underestimate your own unique talents and abilities; they have the power to shape the future of our schools and create a better learning culture that our students need and deserve. Everyone has the ability to lead in some capacity, and *our schools—and the kids who are being shaped inside them—need more educators to embrace this challenge.*[1]

Leadership is defined by action, not by one's title on a business card. In life, your success is intimately tied to your actions.

Stop & REFLECT

When you think of the words "school leader," who comes to mind? What characteristics does that individual consistently display?

From my experience, quite often, especially in toxic environments, educators will talk about "a lack of leadership," which is often paired with comments about "low morale." Toxic school cultures are real. Toxic, egocentric, self-serving "leadership" is real. Innovation will not thrive in these school and classroom cultures, and risk-taking will be minimal. In these spaces, it is ultimately the students who have the most to lose.

IN LIFE, YOUR SUCCESS IS INTIMATELY TIED TO YOUR ACTIONS.

This cycle of toxicity will continue until hearts change or other leaders rise.

Some of the most dynamic school leaders I've ever worked with are perhaps not whom you'd expect. It has been the third-year teacher that runs through walls for kids every single day. It has been the support staff member who earns far less than she deserves yet is a backbone to the building and knows every child within it. It has been the thirty-five-year veteran, teaching her last year but making every day count. She'd been teaching second grade for twenty years, but she still recognized that her students only had one year in second grade, so she did whatever it took for them to have their best year yet.

The best leaders, whether in the classroom or the office, don't believe it is someone else's responsibility to make great things happen. The best leaders don't believe it is someone else's responsibility to make their schools a great place to work. The best leaders don't point the finger outward before they point the finger at themselves and examine inward.

Leadership starts with you.

Regardless of your role, regardless of your position, if you work in a school, *you are a leader for kids*. If you work in a toxic environment, you have two choices: maximize blame and minimize impact or maximize impact and minimize blame. If you work in a toxic environment and the perceived consensus is that the toxicity is due to one person, what would happen if you and every other adult in the building did everything in their power to make yours the greatest school on the planet in which to work? Some may call it a utopian thought. But why?

Toxic environments are real, but to move out of that environment, we must own our parts in the learning culture, regardless of our titles.

So much of the role of leadership comes down to one word—*mindset*. It's easier to point the finger than it is to take responsibility. It's easier to make an excuse than to fight an uphill battle. It's easier to hide than it is to rise in the midst of uncertainty.

If you want your school to have great leadership, it begins with you. If I want my organization to have great leadership, it begins with me. Our mindsets, our actions, and our circles of influence can move us forward. We can't do it for others. We can only do it for ourselves.

Every one of us is responsible for our workplace cultures. Each of us contributes to it. Each of us either builds it up or tears it down, even just a little bit, each day. Right now, your school's culture perfectly aligns with the mindset and actions of the adults in your building. If we want things to change, we must look inward before we look around us. We must move forward if we want the whole group to move forward; otherwise, we're simply solidifying the foundation of the status quo.

RIGHT NOW, YOUR SCHOOL'S CULTURE PERFECTLY ALIGNS WITH THE MINDSET AND ACTIONS OF THE ADULTS IN YOUR BUILDING.

While toxic school cultures and poor leadership are very real, so are the countless schools and districts that people flock to each day. These are places of joy, places where both students and staff want to be. These are places where leaders take responsibility and model the way, where the adults do whatever it takes for students to thrive. These places aren't created by one person. Cultures of innovation are the culmination of action-oriented leadership by many inside an organization.

Where leaders rise, kids win.

The top levels of leadership of an organization set the tone for the culture within. In toxic cultures, innovation will not and cannot thrive. In cultures of innovation, the unthinkable becomes possible. It's a superintendent and her team who set the tone for a district, principal for her school, and a teacher for his classroom.

"Culture," as defined by Merriam-Webster, is "the set of shared attitudes, values, goals, and practices that characterizes an institution or organization."

Take a moment to consider the following questions:

> What are the shared attitudes of those in your school or district?

> What shared values are consistent among those that work with you?

> What shared goals are in place and owned by those on your team?

> What types of practices are most consistent?

> Do the attitudes and practices in your school propel or hinder learning that is *personal* and *authentic*?

CULTURES OF INNOVATION ARE THE CULMINATION OF ACTION-ORIENTED LEADERSHIP BY MANY INSIDE AN ORGANIZATION.

For learning to be *personal* and *authentic*, an inclusive culture must be in place so students know they belong, regardless of differences they may have from those around them. In these cultures of innovation, the adults model the desired behaviors, and both staff and students understand that every person and every interaction matters.

Try This

> Hire by committee. Give teachers a voice in who their next colleague will be.

> Provide mentors for new teachers for their first three years, giving veteran teachers opportunities to build capacity in the next generation of the profession.

> Empower teachers to plan and lead professional learning throughout the year. If most professional learning is top-down, there will be significant resistance and, quite often, minimal impact.

> Set aside time for reflection at all levels. Reflecting on experience propels growth.

> Principals: Sometimes the best things happen when we get out of the way and let our people run! Build capacity and give them the opportunity to do so.

> Educational leaders are not simply those that have chosen the career field, but are those who send their children to school every day with their best hopes and expectations. Intentionally engage families and give them the opportunity to lead!

EVERY INTERACTION MATTERS

"People will forget what you said, people will forget what you did, but people will never forget how you made them feel."

—MAYA ANGELOU

Make It Stick

"As a leader, every point of contact is a moment of transformation. Look for ways to add value to each person you come in contact with each day. Be a source of energy and inspiration through your actions and your speech."

—Sanée Bell junior high school principal, Texas

Each summer, I have the privilege to work alongside thousands of educators to help kick off their school year. The energy surrounding these days is infectious. For me, one day from the summer of 2018 stands head and shoulders above the rest. It wasn't what happened while on-site that became a moment in time that I will never forget; it was what happened on my trip back home.

Like many other days, I was on the go and running non-stop. Part of my world entails spending countless nights away from home, in hotels scattered around the country while flying from place to place. That afternoon was similar to so many I'd had before.

After opening for a district that morning and rushing back to the San Diego airport, I dropped my rental car off and hopped on the airport shuttle bus. But I'd hopped on the wrong shuttle bus. Being at airports non-stop doesn't prevent me from making careless mistakes at them. Just before the driver pulled away, I grabbed my stuff, hopped off, and ran to the other shuttle; this time, it was the right one. As we drove toward the airport, I did what I've done hundreds of times: I looked down at my phone, made sure I was checked in, looked up my gate, and figured out how much time I had until I boarded. A few minutes later, our crowded bus full of travelers disembarked in what seemed to be complete chaos.

I moved through the large crowd and followed signs to Terminal 2. Upon arriving, I looked around and saw all of the airlines for my terminal, except for the one I was taking, American Airlines. Flying so much each year, I'm entirely comfortable in airports, but for a few moments in this one, I felt alone and lost. I looked around and finally asked someone for help. An older gentleman pointed me toward the opposite end and said, "Didn't you see it? It's on the other side. You have to go all the way back down there." I thanked him and went on my way, walking quickly back through baggage claim and again through the masses of people toward the other side of the terminal.

About halfway through the crowd, I noticed a man about my age. I could tell he seemed a bit lost and appeared to be looking for someone or something. He was holding a cane and was wearing unique glasses. I remember thinking to myself that he was probably trying to locate his bag. I also thought about how challenging that must be if he was alone and was, in fact, blind like I had assumed.

I kept walking and eventually walked right by him, glancing back down at my phone.

Consumed with my own craziness, all that was on my own plate, the calls I had to make, and the work I had to get done, I continued walking toward the security checkpoint. At one point, I turned back to glance at the man who had caught my attention and noticed that he continued to stand alone. It was clear he felt lost, just as I had a few minutes prior on the other side of the terminal.

I started to feel sick to my stomach.

A few hours before, I'd had the opportunity to encourage almost one thousand educators who give their all for kids every day at a Southern California opening day. In part of my talk that morning, I was challenging them on building relationships and the responsibility of building and owning the culture in their schools. I shared how even the smallest interaction can make someone's day and be an encouragement, how showing someone you care and that they matter can be life-changing.

That morning I was hoping to tug at their hearts by helping them truly understand their lifelong impacts and how their fingerprints would be left forever on the children they serve. This afternoon, however, it was my own heart tugging back at me. The further I walked, the more like a hypocrite I felt. Here I had just been challenging others to make every interaction count, and there I had just walked right past someone with obvious physical needs who could use some help.

So I humbly listened to that little voice inside my head, and I turned around.

I hustled back over to the man who was still standing there, looking around, and it reminded me of how I had felt only minutes before, but I had been able to see where I was. I walked up to him and simply said, "Hi, my name is Tom. You look like you need some help. Can I help you with something?"

"I'm not sure where I am," he said. I asked him which airline he had just flown and if he was trying to get his bag.

"I can't remember which one it was," he said.

I started to realize he needed a bit more help than which direction to head or how to find his bag. I looked around and saw an information desk by one of the exit doors, figuring those at the booth might be able to help. I asked the man his name, to which he replied, "Scott," and then I invited him to put his hand on my shoulder to go figure out where he needed to go. As we started walking together, I asked if he had a boarding pass so we could help figure out where he needed to go.

Scott responded, "I think it started with a U. I don't remember. And I came from up north."

Over the next few minutes, the attendant at the information desk helped us figure out which plane Scott came in on and which carousel his baggage would arrive. The attendant asked, "Scott, was it the United flight from San Francisco?"

He responded, "Oh. Yes, sir. That's it. Thank you." The attendant then pointed to the far end of the building, exactly where I had just asked for my own directions.

Scott turned to me and said, "Thank you for helping me." Still feeling bad that I had walked right by him the first time, like hundreds of others, I asked if I could help him get down to the other end safely and help him get his bag.

As we began to navigate the crowd, Scott paused and turned toward me. "I'm really sorry. I have a hard time knowing where I am sometimes, and it's easy to forget things. It's not that I'm blind; my brain just doesn't function right," he said.

I replied, "No problem, Scott, let's get you there safely. I'm glad to help."

After glancing at my phone to see how much time I had to get to my gate, I asked Scott what his bag looked like. He struggled to get the word camouflage out. He then said, "It's a military color."

Having a dad that served in the Marines and having tremendous respect for those who protect our freedom, I paused and asked, "Scott, are you in the military?"

Scott stopped walking in the middle of the crowded room and pointed to his hat. "Purple Heart" was embroidered on it. I had completely missed it, both the first time I walked by him and during our few minutes of interaction.

Scott slowly began, "It happened in Mosul. It's a place in Iraq, if you've never heard of it. I was Delta Force. It's part of the army."

My heart stopped. I started to anticipate where he was going with his story.

He continued. "It was a beautiful day like today, except it was much hotter. Maybe one hundred and thirty degrees and, trust me, that's really hot." He laughed. "I can still smell the air from that day. My team was helping a family in the city. We were keeping these women and children safe because there were a lot of bad guys in the area."

I'm not ashamed to admit that it was about that moment I had to hold back tears.

"We thought the bad guys had left. A while later, I went to check if they had and walked out the front door." He paused again. "That's when it happened. I got shot." He turned and pointed to the left side of his head. "We were trying to help protect them. I didn't see it coming. I didn't see it coming."

As Scott relived a few minutes of a life-changing day, the last day of what he had always known, I became emotional thinking how only a few minutes prior, I was so self-consumed in all I had to do that I had walked right by this amazing, courageous man.

Scott continued. "But it's okay. I'm going to be okay. The problem is the bullet is still in my brain. It's right there." He pointed to a spot on his head. "The doctors say they can't move it and can't take it out, and it needs to stay in there. But I'm okay. This is just my new life."

The floodgates opened. My tears flowed as I stood listening to the story of someone whom I had completely ignored just a few minutes earlier.

We made our way over to baggage claim, his hand still on my shoulder. As we worked our way through the crowd, I asked about his story and where he was from. Scott shared that he had grown up in Texas. He talked about his family and how he joined the military to help people in need and how he always liked helping other people.

I grabbed his camouflage bag off the conveyor belt, and we moved to the place outside where his dad was going to pick him up. As we waited, he turned to me and said, "I don't understand why you wanted to help. Most people just walk right by."

His words sent chills through me.

My heart sank because I had been one of the people who walked right by him. I was the one who couldn't take a few moments to help someone. I had been all-consumed with myself. I'd been too busy and too preoccupied with my own needs to realize that I was in the presence of a hero.

"Hey, Scott, it's not every day that I get to meet an American hero," I said. "Can we take a picture so I can remember you and your story? I want to tell my kids about you. I want them to grow up and understand what true sacrifice means and what a hero really looks like . . . and it looks just like you."

Scott nodded and said, "I'd be honored to, sir."

As his dad approached, Scott stuck his hand out and said, "Thanks for being a friend, Tom."

Feeling like I didn't even deserve to carry this hero's luggage and with tears streaming down my face, I could only get out, "No, thank you, Scott."

It was truly an honor to be in Scott's presence and have the privilege of carrying his bags while helping him safely get to where he needed to be. It was an honor that I will never forget.

For me, those moments reaffirmed how every interaction matters.

In our schools and in our classrooms, every interaction matters. We must also understand that every interaction is an opportunity to make an impact on those around us. A single interaction can change a person's life forever.

WHEN YOU WALK INTO THE FACULTY ROOM, DO YOU BUILD THE ENERGY UP? OR DO YOU SUCK THE AIR RIGHT OUT?

As kids walk by us in the hallway, how do we react? Are we looking at our phones or looking into their hearts? When we see a child in need or one who appears to be lost or one who seems to have a heavy heart, do we keep walking? Or do we pause our own worlds for a few moments to help lift someone else's higher?

As we engage with students in the classroom, what do our everyday interactions look like? How can we ensure that we make every interaction count? How can our daily interactions show kids how much they matter?

As an educator, every day is an opportunity to have an amazing impact on those around you. Even a chance interaction can be life-changing, just as meeting Scott was for me that August afternoon.

To create cultures of innovation where learning is *personal* and *authentic*, we must recognize that every interaction matters.

Stop & REFLECT

Think of a recent interaction that was *personal* for you. How was that interaction *authentic* in nature? What type of impact did it have on you?

We must own our actions. We must own our mindsets. We must own the opportunities that we take and those we pass on. We must own our roles in creating the cultures our kids need to thrive.

When you walk into the faculty room, do you build the energy up? Or do you suck the air right out? If asked, would those around you compare you to a faucet that pours into the lives of others and adds to the existing energy? Or would they say you're more like a drain, where the energy and momentum go to disappear?

What flows out of you?

We must own our abilities to create the cultures our kids need to thrive by making every interaction count. When done consistently over time, it is these interactions, these moments, that build trust.

Try This

> Keep a personal journal in your desk or digitally. At the end of each day, spend three to four minutes reflecting on which interactions you feel were most impactful that day. At the start of each week, take a few minutes to read and reflect on your impact from the previous week.

> Find a colleague whom you admire who "makes every interaction count." Tell that person why you enjoy working together.

> Keep a private "Interactions Checklist" where you can informally keep track of meaningful interactions with your students (or staff). Over time, reflect on those you haven't connected with and go out of your way to do so.

BUILDING TRUST

"Trust takes years to build, seconds to break, and forever to repair."

—UNKNOWN

Whatever takes time and energy to build can also be shattered in a moment. Without it, little positive progress can be made. With it, unbreakable bonds can be secured. Learning cultures depend on it.

Trust, the foundation of all interactions, dictates the speed at which progress in our classrooms and schools can be made. Leadership works at the speed of trust. Collaboration works at the speed of trust. Transformation works at the speed of trust. School and classroom cultures where *personal* and *authentic* learning flourishes are built at the speed of trust.

What is it that you do to intentionally build trust in your classroom or school? This isn't a one-time activity or something that gets checked off the list on the first day of school. How do you build trust consistently over time?

SCHOOL AND CLASSROOM CULTURES WHERE *PERSONAL* AND *AUTHENTIC* LEARNING FLOURISHES ARE BUILT AT THE SPEED OF TRUST.

As educators, we process things with our minds but often make decisions with our hearts. We cannot forget that our students do the same. It is through trust that we can build relationships—the foundation of *personal* and *authentic* learning cultures. It's no secret that students learn from people they love. This love comes from a sense of safety, security, and knowing one is cared for in the process. It is trust that stabilizes and solidifies these in our daily interactions.

Before trust can become an unwavering thread of classroom culture, educators must learn to trust themselves. Putting trust in ourselves comes from a sense of knowing that we are worth it.

Make It Stick

"To help build a learning culture, play a song of the day (that students enjoy) as students enter in the morning and in between classes."

—Micah Shippee, middle school teacher, New York

Putting such trust in ourselves comes from us being cognizant of our own needs—our self-care. Self-care allows us to refuel so we can continue the work we are so passionate about.

We can only maximize building trust with others when we take care of ourselves first. Doing "whatever it takes" for kids does not mean running yourself ragged in the process. Doing "whatever it takes" for kids means being able to put yourself in position to advocate for those traditionally underserved, to bring passion to your content area, or have a quiet moment with a child in need, and be your best while doing so. We must take care of ourselves as educators to maximize our effectiveness during the most challenging moments. We spend time every day recharging our phones but often go months without recharging ourselves.

Everyone who has flown in an airplane has heard the standard pre-flight announcements (or at least have been present as they've occurred). During these announcements, the flight attendants will instruct passengers on what to do in an emergency situation. It goes something like this:

"In case of a loss of cabin pressure, oxygen masks above your seat will deploy. Please place the mask on yourself first before helping others."

WE SPEND TIME EVERY DAY RECHARGING OUR PHONES BUT OFTEN GO MONTHS WITHOUT RECHARGING OURSELVES.

Many have used this as an analogy for self-care, and I understand the point being made: In order to assist others, we have to take care of ourselves first. However, I think it's essential to rethink this common analogy and understand that this comparison actually points out a common issue, as well an opportunity for reflection.

The analogy illustrates what we as humans, and as educators, often do. We regularly give so much to others that we forget to take care of ourselves until, like the plane, we are in freefall and forced to put on the oxygen mask. Oftentimes, we don't take care of ourselves until the doctor gives us the bad news or our spouse shares her heart or we discover the part of life we've been missing out on has started to fade away.

If we as educators wait for an extreme emergency to put on our oxygen masks, we've already lost a part of our effectiveness. We've all heard personal reflections after life-altering incidents, such as the loss of a loved one, and talks of how experiences

Make It Stick

"Commit to a daily self-care streak! Select an action geared toward your own health needs and refuse to release this streak for the duration you set. Be flexible in the way it fits into each day and tenacious about making the space to restore and renew the best version of you."

—Sarah Johnson, educator, Wisconsin

force people to reprioritize, slow down, spend time with those they love, or focus on healing themselves.

As humans, we've all felt the highest of the highs, those moments where we feel invincible and on top of the world. We can also all relate to those moments where we struggle—those moments in which it seems impossible to go on, where fear or self-doubt has left us feeling paralyzed.

Educators are some of the most dedicated, hard-working, loving, and selfless people on the planet. Yet sometimes this type of servant's heart comes with a fault and at the expense of those we love the most. Serving others does not mean giving until you have nothing left. When running on an empty heart, one's effectiveness is diminished.

An empty heart leads to a lack of trust in oneself. You can't pour water from an empty cup, and you can't pour love from an empty heart. If we are going to invest in the lives of others, we must continually invest in ourselves.

We are worth it! You are worth it! Our kids are worth it!

Self-care empowers us to invest in others and build meaningful trust as the bonds are forming. How can educators build trust with those around them? For me, during my second week teaching, it was my superintendent who modeled a first step in trust building.

WE MUST TAKE CARE OF OURSELVES AS EDUCATORS TO MAXIMIZE OUR EFFECTIVENESS DURING THE MOST CHALLENGING MOMENTS.

That afternoon, students had returned from lunch, and my class was getting started with reading time. As my students were listening to the read-aloud that afternoon, I glanced to my left and saw my superintendent, Dr. Scanlon, standing in my classroom doorway with a smile on his face.

"Mr. Murray, do you have a moment?" he asked.

My heart stopped. Here I was, in only my second week of teaching, and the superintendent was asking to see me in the hallway. I remember wondering if this was the beginning of the "go get your box" type of conversation.

Had I done something wrong? Was I not doing things the way the district wanted? Was I not meeting expectations?

I told my students that I needed to step into the hall for just a moment. That moment turned out to be less than thirty seconds.

Dr. Scanlon reached out to shake my hand. "Hey, Tom, it's good to see you."

"Good Afternoon, Dr. Scanlon," I replied. He could probably hear the nerves in my voice.

He went on. "Tom, yesterday while at the district office, I overheard someone sharing how you had the kids outside doing team-building activities during your very first week. I wanted to come over to say, don't ever stop trying new things and don't ever stop stepping out of your comfort zone for your students. I'm impressed that during your first week, you were already trying new things with your kids. Keep trying new things and know that we're here if you need anything. Have a great rest of your afternoon and keep up the great work."

Dr. Scanlon smiled, shook my hand again, and walked back down the hallway.

I'm not sure if my hands were raised walking back into the classroom as if I had just run through the end point of a marathon, but I remember feeling like I was on top of the world. That moment took less than thirty seconds, yet today, almost two decades later, I can show you where my feet were standing.

The power of moments. The power of *authentic* words of affirmation. The power of trust building.

> ## Make It Stick
>
> "If we are going to ask students at the beginning of the school year for information to help us build relationships, then we need to follow up with those students about their responses. To build trust, we need to repeat that activity many times throughout the year."
>
> —Jimmy Casas, educator, Iowa

Stop & REFLECT

What have these interactions looked and felt like for you as an educator? How have those moments encouraged you to do the same for others?

In life, we have all experienced these types of moments. Such moments can empower us to feel as if we can tackle whatever comes our way. Yet moments that scar our hearts can also become ingrained in our minds and cause self-doubt that is difficult to overcome. That's the fine line with trust.

I'd learn over time that, for Dr. Scanlon, this type of brief interaction was part of who he was, part of the way he modeled leadership. He understood the power of genuine words of affirmation. He understood that to build a team, you must first build relationships. He understood that trust was the root of a *personal* and *authentic* learning culture.

Which student in your classroom needs these types of interactions the most? Which teacher on your team would benefit the most from a *personal* and *authentic* interaction like this?

In our classrooms, *trust* isn't a single word. It isn't built from a single moment in time. Trust is the culmination of the intentional actions, reactions, attitudes, and moments we share with those around us.

For empowerment to be possible, trust must first solidify one's confidence. Without trust, we have very little, if anything at all. Without trust, *personal* and *authentic* learning isn't feasible.

How can we build trust with those around us?

1. **Be Honest**—You'll make mistakes along the way; own them when they happen. Trust is rooted in honesty.
2. **Be Authentic**—If people don't feel they see the real you, you cannot build trust.
3. **Be Kind**—Kindness doesn't mean we're always "nice" to people. It means that we treat every situation with compassion.
4. **Be Empathetic**—Every one of us is facing battles in our hearts and in our minds. Some of us face more than others. Empathy is the ability to understand and share the feelings of another.
5. **Be Reliable**—Follow through on the things you say you'll do. A mismatch between what you say you'll do and what you actually do leads to doubt in others.
6. **Be Consistent**—We build trust through consistency and steady actions that occur over time.

7. **Be Competent**—If people don't believe you have the capacity to get the work done, they won't trust you in the process. Such competency comes from studying the actions of those more skilled than we are and learning through practice.

Knowing that every interaction matters and that trust is the foundation of relationships, we have the opportunity to invest in others every day and build the bonds that become the roots of success. No interaction is too small, and time spent investing in the lives of others is never wasted.

A 2018 study conducted with middle school students directed teachers to change one small part of their practice. The practice didn't cost money, didn't take extensive training, and didn't add to curricular needs. Ultimately, the practice increased academic engagement by twenty percentage points and decreased disruptive behavior by nine percentage points, "potentially adding an hour of engagement over the course of a five-hour instructional day."[2]

TRUST IS THE CULMINATION OF THE INTENTIONAL ACTIONS, REACTIONS, ATTITUDES, AND MOMENTS WE SHARE WITH THOSE AROUND US.

What was this profound practice or latest technique? What could have such an impact on student engagement and behavior?

Positive, intentional greetings at the door before the class period began. Yes, really.

Teachers who spend time welcoming students to their classrooms establish a sense that students matter and that they are worth our time, which in turn invests in their social and emotional love tank. Standing at the door and welcoming students also symbolizes that we as teachers will come to you as students. We'll meet you where you are. We're here just for you.

The study, *Positive Greetings at the Door: Evaluation of a Low-Cost, High-Yield Proactive Classroom Management Strategy*,[3] concluded that positive greetings to start the time together work because they "establish a positive classroom climate in which students feel a sense of connection and belonging." The authors of the study state, "This is particularly important considering the research demonstrating that achievement motivation is often a byproduct of social belonging and that pre-session attention can establish momentum for desired behavior . . . . Together, these core features of the PGD strategy [Positive Greetings at the Door] help create behavioral momentum for behavioral engagement, maximize instructional time, and prevent the occurrence of problem behaviors that interfere with learning."

NO INTERACTION IS TOO SMALL, AND TIME SPENT INVESTING IN THE LIVES OF OTHERS IS NEVER WASTED.

Stop & REFLECT

What do the first few moments of each school day or class period look like for you? What are you intentional about during that time?

It is moments like these—the nonverbal interpersonal interactions, such as a high-five, a smile, a thumbs up, or a friendly handshake—that can support a student's sense of social belonging. Such belonging creates a sense of worth, an inherent sense of value. This worth, in turn, helps develop a mindset and the confidence that anything is possible.

If we are going to make learning more *personal* and *authentic*, there must be a strong bond of trust. For the learning experience to transform, both educators and students must be willing to take risks. When trust empowers risk-taking, deeper levels of learning can flourish.

Try This

> Ask students about their interests and passions and be intentional in highlighting those in conversation and activities over the course of the year.

> Avoid speaking poorly of others. People begin to wonder what you'll say about them behind a closed door.

> Practice what you preach. Saying one thing to students, yet modeling another, is one of the quickest ways to shatter trust in the classroom.

> Principals: Try buying your teachers well-designed business cards. This can show you value them and see them as professionals.

RISK-TAKING

"Twenty years from now, you will be more disappointed by the things you didn't do than by the ones you did. So throw off the bowlines, sail away from the safe harbor, catch the trade winds in your sails. Explore. Dream. Discover."

−MARK TWAIN

It is our fear of failure that can be the most paralyzing. It is that first step that is often the hardest. Without trust in oneself and the ability to overcome our fears, risk-taking may feel nearly impossible.

How do you define *fear*?

Forget	**F**ace
Everything	**E**verything
And	**A**nd
Run	**R**ise

Credit: Zig Ziglar

Oprah Winfrey is known as one of the most successful entrepreneurs in the world. Over the course of her career, she has built a brand legacy from the ground up and launched a variety of philanthropic organizations to provide opportunities for others. In 2018, Winfrey was recognized as the only African-American woman on the *Forbes* billionaires list with a net worth of almost three billion dollars.[4] Unlike others on the list, Winfrey has persevered through adversity to earn all that she has and has been forced to take risks along the way. Born into poverty in rural Mississippi to a teenaged single mother, she was later raised in Milwaukee, Wisconsin. Following a difficult upbringing, Winfrey was sent to live with the man she refers to as her father and left the inner-city to move to Tennessee, where she later would attend Tennessee State University on a scholarship.

By the age of nineteen, Winfrey entered the television industry and was working as the co-anchor for the local evening news. Yet in time, Winfrey was demoted from her job as a news anchor because she wasn't "fit for television." She persevered and worked at her craft. She gained confidence and then ultimately risked it all.

In the mid-1980s, Winfrey decided to put her financial security on the line by signing a deal to host her own television program. Later, *The Oprah Winfrey Show* would go on to become the highest-rated program of its kind, ever.[5]

Make It Stick

"As a superintendent, I would encourage teachers to take risks and have fun. Find things that you and your students are passionate about and explore. Be the advocate for change and serve as a role model. It's OKay if things don't work out as you expect. It's OKay for things to be messy once in a while, as long as you learn from your mistakes and make the necessary adjustments."

—Jerry Almendarez, superintendent, California

Whether in show business or in education, amazing new things don't happen from places of comfort. Taking calculated risks is how big things happen. Calculated risk-taking requires both courage and competence as well as the ability to welcome the uncertainty that comes with the journey. This isn't about being careless. It's about intentionally stepping out of our comfort zones to make the unthinkable possible.

For learning to be *personal* and *authentic*, those involved must take risks throughout the process. If we as teachers expect our students to take risks, we must model the type of risk-taking we want to see. If administrators expect teachers to take risks, they must first model the way and nurture a learning culture where risk-taking will thrive.

Stop & REFLECT

Whether for your students or your teachers, how do you model risk-taking for those you lead?

Everything we are sure of, we once had to step out and learn. Many times, the things we dream possible are found on the other side of fear.

Our human nature drifts to the old, toward the things that are familiar to us. Our brains are wired to seek such comfort and familiarity. Yet, success won't fall in your lap. It must be fearlessly pursued.

As educators, we must be willing to make mistakes. We must be willing to blur the boundaries of our comfort zone and model our *personal* and *authentic* path forward for our students. To develop the new and to spark the innovative, some type of cognitive disinhibition is necessary. When we take a risk and make a mistake, we often find ourselves being creative and thinking differently to alter where we are so we can get to where we want to be. At the intersection of these moments, new and better things can emerge.

Stop & REFLECT

What have you wanted to try in your classroom or school but have been hesitant to do? What support do you need to make it happen?

It starts by taking one step. Then another. Then another. Once there, you begin to realize that there's typically not a whole lot of traffic once you've gone the extra mile.

Great, otherwise unexpected, opportunities will often arise in risk-taking. Embracing such a mindset simultaneously helps you overcome a natural fear of failure and develop the confidence to help you thrive.

Our greatest hope has far more power than our biggest fear. The same can be said for the students we lead. For learning to be *personal* and *authentic*, we must create cultures of risk-taking for all learners big and small so we can overcome our fears and passionately pursue what our kids need.

Try This

> Before we ask students to step out of their comfort zones and try new things, we must be willing to do that ourselves. Model your thought process to your students as you try something new.

> Be willing to show vulnerability in front of your students. Know that your students can't relate to people who come across as being perfect. Be willing to share your mistakes along the way.

> Include diverse stories of people who overcame adversity throughout the year. Have students choose a person from history that they admire and share the story of how that person overcame fear to become the success story that we know.

A CLOSER LOOK

For a deeper dive into Chapter 2 as well as free tools, resources, and study guide questions, visit **thomascmurray.com/AuthenticEDU2**.

chapter 3

UNDERSTANDING THE STORY
INSIDE EACH LEARNER

STORIES CREATE COMMUNITY, ENABLE US
TO SEE THROUGH THE EYES OF OTHER PEOPLE,
AND OPEN US TO THE CLAIMS OF OTHERS.

—PETER FORBES

W hat's your story? What are the life experiences that are core to who you are? What are the things in life that have molded your lens and impacted the way you see the world? How does your unique story impact your work as an educator? The use of story, one of the most powerful tools since the beginning of mankind, gives insight into all those who seek to understand.

The next time you have a few extra minutes, find a class composite from a previous school year. As you look at the class picture, what comes to mind? As you look at their faces, what is it you remember? What were the life stories that made those students who they were? How did those stories impact them as learners? My guess is you may not remember that particular picture day, but you will remember many stories behind the moments spent with those kids.

There is immense power in understanding a story. Such insight can help us make new connections. Such context can help us see things differently and, at times, make visible the why behind something we previously struggled to understand.

START WITH WHY

"When you know your why, your what has more impact, because you are walking in or towards your purpose."
— MICHAEL JR.

"Why are we learning this?"
"Why do I have to do that?"
"Why?"
Sound familiar?

Humans crave a defined sense of purpose. Naturally, we seek to understand and make personal connections to the world around us. With such connections a necessity, as we move to create *personal* and *authentic* learning experiences, we must focus on and understand *the why*.

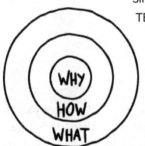

Simon Sinek unveiled his "Golden Circle" in his TEDx Talk, "How Great Leaders Inspire Action." Sinek explained that most businesses think, act, and communicate in the exact same way, from the outside in. Starting with "what" and moving to "how" has become the norm in the way businesses and people communicate. It's no secret that the same holds true in our educational paradigm as well.

According to Sinek, "The inspired leaders and the inspired organizations, regardless of their size, and regardless of their industry, all think, act, and communicate, from the inside out."[1] He went on to highlight examples of those who altered the course of human history, such as Martin Luther King, Jr., Steve Jobs, and the Wright Brothers.

Whether it was Wilbur and Orville Wright making four brief flights at Kitty Hawk with the first powered aircraft in 1903, Martin Luther King, Jr. delivering his "I Have a Dream" speech on the steps of the Lincoln Memorial in 1963, or Steve Jobs revealing "an iPod, a phone, and an internet communicator" called the iPhone in 2007, each world-changing moment began with why. These leaders may have been from different generations and had little in common, but they were all driven by their personal causes and senses of purpose. Each of these individuals was brilliant, but it was the way they passionately led with their why that separated these icons from others with similar ambitions.

$Stop$ & REFLECT

What is your why? What is your purpose? Why do you do what you do?

"All kids have greatness hidden inside them. It is the job of an educator to help them find and unleash it."
—ERIC SHENINGER

Many often miss the fact that Sinek's work with the Golden Circle is supported by neuroscience. The outer ring of the Golden Circle (the *what*) correlates with the outer section of the human brain, known as the neocortex. This section of the brain is responsible for conscious thought, language, and higher-order brain functions like sensory perception and motor commands. It has also been shown to be central to sleep, memory, and learning processes. This is where rational thought and the understanding of facts occur.

The middle two concentric circles (the *how* and the *why*) correlate to the middle section of the brain known as the limbic system. This is the system that supports behavior, emotion, and motivation. It's the portion of the brain where one's intuition comes from and where long-term memory resides.

In understanding the basics of how the human brain works, we know that we must connect with the limbic system to increase motivation and change behavior. It's ultimately why social-emotional learning, discussed in Chapter 5, is central to valuing, recognizing, and appreciating the whole child.

Starting with *why* is imperative as we work to shift the learning paradigm in our classrooms. It is the *why* that drives us and the *why* that can change our behaviors. Understanding the *why* makes a shift in practice possible. Consistently living out the *why* leads to a sustainable change in experience.

So why shift practice to a more *personal* and *authentic* experience for today's modern learners?

The educational parallel of the Golden Circle to what we know about how the human brain works is evident. The limbic system is involved when something is *personal* and *authentic* to one's experience. In turn, motivation increases, emotions are tapped, and long-term memory improves. Creating experiences that are *personal* and *authentic* in nature also helps us respect the fact that we are teaching the most diverse generation in history. Each learner is unique, having been molded by his or her life story, and has incredible potential. Each learner in every classroom and every school is an amazing opportunity.

Learning that is *personal* and *authentic* respects and recognizes that each person has a valuable story. Each administrator. Each teacher. Each support staff member. Each student. Each story is unique and beautiful in its own way. Each story is filled with varying degrees of hope and happiness mixed with varying levels of doubt and sadness. Each of these stories evolves over time, is found at the core of who we are, and shades the lens of how we see the world around us.

Each story is *personal*. Each story is *authentic*.

Each winter, people will discuss how "no two snowflakes are alike." Although the process of the formation of snow may be scientifically identical, upon landing, each snowflake has its own unique identity. While many similarities may exist among different snowflakes, each one has characteristics that differentiate it from the rest. So if made in the same way, how does each snowflake become unique? Each snowflake takes a different journey from inception to its resting place, affecting its shape, size, and, ultimately, its identity.

There is a clear correlation between humans and snowflakes, as each of us is on a unique journey through life that alters who we are along the way. From our earliest interactions, we become uniquely knit at our cores. Our beliefs. Our perceptions. Our mindsets. Our personal stories amplify our cores.

Stop & REFLECT

What's your story? Which of your life experiences have been central to how you see the world?

Understanding one's story fuels deeper connections that are personal in nature. Understanding one's beautiful uniqueness amplifies authenticity. Being *personal* and *authentic* makes connections to the heart, which opens vast opportunities for the mind. For learning to be both *personal* and *authentic*, understanding the story within each learner is essential. A child's story defines the context in which his or her learning occurs.

Kids are not data points. Kids are not test scores. Kids will never be "standard." Although data and meaningful assessments may be helpful measures in understanding how to support a student, *they must never define a student*. To do so would be incredibly short-sighted and a disservice to the unique gifts and abilities inside each child. To do so would not accurately represent the meaningful story inside each learner.

To be *personal* and *authentic*, we must be driven by a why that values each learner as an individual—one with a unique story that makes them who they are and provides the lens through which they see and understand the world.

A CHILD'S STORY DEFINES THE CONTEXT IN WHICH HIS OR HER LEARNING OCCURS.

Make It Stick

"Celebrate students the way they want to be celebrated. Pizza parties don't mean the same to everyone."

—Abbey Futrell
assistant superintendent,
North Carolina

IN PRACTICE

MATT MILLER, SUPERINTENDENT, LAKOTA LOCAL SCHOOL DISTRICT, OHIO

Why? I'll tell you why.

Why? *Why* do we work in our chosen profession? *Why* do we decide to never stop learning? *Why* do we never stop getting butterflies about another "first day" of school? (I'll be on my forty-third coming up this fall.) *Why* do we choose a profession where we sometimes get second guessed by those "outside of the arena"? *Why* do we go into a profession where our numbers seem to be getting smaller year after year?

Why? I'll tell you *why*. In our chosen profession, no matter our role, and no matter the issue, our victories are big. There are no small victories for our kids or for our teachers. When I think about it—and when you think about it—our why is most likely the same. It comes down to one factor: relationships. Finding our *why* through building relationships can take time, but when we find it, things change. We change. Our *why* becomes our focus. When we understand that relationships drive the *why*, we find our motivation, our calling makes sense, and we become relentlessly actionable.

When *why* is the driver, educators understand that there is an ebb and flow and different layers to the relationships with students and with our peers. Through our evolving why, we learn what motivation works for our students and how that motivation helps us with an uptick in fostering and tending to true, engaging relationships.

One of the best reasons for discovering the *why* as educators is that we can share our *why* with those around us. How powerful is it when we tell a group of students, or just one student, that they are our *why*? They are the reason we went into teaching, and they are the reason we bring our best into our classrooms every single day. It's positively transformational. I've seen it, and it's unapologetically moving. When we tell kids they are the why, we show them the impact they have on us. We become vulnerable, we become real, we become connected, and we become engaged. Relationships are the *why*, and we must work on them every single chance we get.

The other overriding reason to share our why with others is that our stories help others grow in their own relationships, their own whys. We become a reminder for others that our relationships with fellow educators and with students need constant work. All of us need our reminders, our reasons to mirror the positives we have going on. Our *why*—the students—is the amplifier we need now in our public schools. When our students know our why, their responses and their engagement move all of us ahead.

Try This

> Have students research a person from history whom they admire. Then have them share who the person was, why they admire that individual, and what, in their view, drove them to be successful.

> Have students write or video produce their why as it pertains to something that they are passionate about.

> When planning, be ready to answer the question, "Why are we learning this?" and then invest a few minutes during the lesson to make the learning connection with students.

THE HIDDEN STORIES OF THOSE AROUND US

"There are no secrets in life, just hidden truths that lie beneath the surface."

—MICHAEL C. HALL

On a cold January morning, I boarded the 7:15 train from 30th Street Station in Philadelphia to head to my office in Washington, D.C. As I regularly do, I found a seat, opened my laptop, turned up the volume in my headphones, and connected to the internet so I could do some work.

Like I do many times each day, I scanned my Twitter feed. While scrolling through, I came across "The Hidden Story," a video shared by the Franklin-Covey company.[2]

For just under three minutes, I sat glued to my screen, watching what would seem to be daily interactions with strangers whose worlds seemed completely separate but connected at the same time.

Had the video not spelled out what was in each character's heart, you would watch what appeared to be people interacting with one another in a small town: a trip to the grocery store, a stop at the pharmacy, and so on. Without seeing the hearts of others on screen, it would resemble every-day life for many. Without seeing the hearts of others on screen, one might wonder what the big deal was or why it was worth taking a few minutes to watch.

The video allows you to see a glimpse into each person's heart. It allows you to see the hidden story within.

> She stayed up all night because her daughter was sick.

> His wife passed away recently, and he's facing life on his own.

> Last night he proposed to his girlfriend, and she said yes!

> Her work hours were reduced, and she's worried about paying her rent.

> He ran out of medication for his depression.

> He just learned his tumor is benign.

"The Hidden Story" video concludes with amazingly powerful words: "If you could see into the hearts of others, feel what they feel, understand their struggles, hopes, fears, and joys . . . how would you treat them? How would your day be different? Just another day?"

Stop & REFLECT

Take a few minutes to reflect on a time in your life where you changed your view on a situation after understanding the story behind it.

I'm not ashamed to say that I was fighting tears as I looked up from my screen in deep reflection. Like I do on most train rides, I was sitting at a table with two seats on each side of it. Sitting across from me was a Black man, probably about fifty years old, dressed professionally. Next to him was a lady of Asian descent, probably mid-forties, also dressed professionally. Sitting next to me was a Caucasian man who appeared to be in his late twenties wearing a hoodie, jeans, and a hat.

It was the first time I even noticed with whom I was sitting. Granted, I had been on the train for only about twenty minutes at this point, but it was the first time I really looked at the people who were with me at the table. With my headphones in and my laptop open, I had been oblivious to my surroundings.

I began to wonder what each of their stories were. Where they were from. Why they were headed to the nation's capital. What was on their hearts? On the outside, we all had noticeable differences, but I'm certain there were so many similarities on the inside.

Reflecting on what I had just seen, I began to think about the times

when my own heart was heavy, but I did my best to fake it. The times my heart was hurting, but life had to go on. Or the greatest of days and feelings of complete joy. The times I had gone through everyday life, smiling on the outside but crying on the inside. The times that some of the hidden stories in the video had been mine. The times I had thought, "If they only knew . . . If my colleagues only understood . . ."

. . . like the days after my wife and I lost our first baby.

. . . followed by the days after we lost our second.

. . . to the days following the birth of our daughter we had longed for.

. . . to the days that followed, learning of her potentially fatal food allergies, after running her into the ER screaming for an EpiPen for the very first time.

. . . to the days following the loss of a family member.

. . . to the days that followed the birth of our little boy.

. . . to the days leading up to and following my dad's surgery, when he had to have a leg removed due to the struggles of his disease.

. . . and on, and on, and on.

If they only knew, maybe they would have understood why I wasn't myself. If they only knew, maybe they would have understood why it wasn't the most important thing on my plate that day.

My hidden story. Your hidden story. Our students' hidden stories.

Stop & **REFLECT**

What hidden stories are inside of you? How do these personal experiences impact you as an educator? How do they impact the way you see the world?

A hidden story is something each of us has, albeit to varying degrees, throughout our lives. It's something that most people we pass in the grocery store, drive past in town, or walk by at work will never know. Yet it's something that will often consume our minds. It's something that will undoubtedly consume our hearts.

Our hidden stories impact each of us every day. Do we choose to see the hidden stories in those around us or just inside ourselves?

As we walk through the halls of our schools, do we seek to understand? When others walk by, do we see faces or do we see hearts? Do we see data points and test scores or do we see the stories and hearts of children? Do we see colleagues first or the people those colleagues are?

DO WE CHOOSE TO SEE THE HIDDEN STORIES IN THOSE AROUND US OR JUST INSIDE OURSELVES?

Do we have empathy for the hidden stories of those around us in our daily interactions? Do we have empathy for the stories we'll never know? Do we have compassion for the pain of hearts we'll never feel?

Being an educator in and of itself is one of the most challenging jobs in the world. Being an educator and showing love for others while your own heart is hurting is an unbelievably courageous act.

The work is hard.
The work is stressful.
The work is emotional.
The work is exhausting.
But our kids are worth it.
Our colleagues are worth it.
We are worth it.

Never give up an opportunity to show those around you that they matter. You may just be the one they've been hoping for.

Learning that is *personal* and *authentic* respects the hidden stories within each individual. When each learner is seen and respected as unique, beauty radiates from within.

Stop & REFLECT

Think of a student you've worked with who had a difficult life story. In what ways did understanding that student's story help you maximize your impact?

Make It Stick

"As we are pressed for time more and more, being asked to fit more things into the school day, the one thing I refuse to give up is my morning check-in routine. Every morning, each kiddo hands me their binder as part of the check-in routine. I love that I get to start off the day saying hello and chatting one-on-one with each of them. You'd be amazed at what you can learn in that short amount of time! Yes, it would be easier and quicker to skip it and have the students pile their binders up for me to look at later, but this way I know I have talked to and connected with each and every one of my kids when the school day begins."

—Meghan Thomas, elementary school teacher, Pennsylvania

Try This

> Be vulnerable and share what makes you who you are. Show empathy so your students feel comfortable doing the same.

> Elementary: Begin the year with a "What Makes Me Special" project and empower students to write and record their personal stories through the use of digital tools. Build on this and create similar experiences throughout the year.

> Secondary: Begin the year with a "To My New Teacher" letter or video production, where students share their stories about what makes them unique. Build on this and create similar experiences throughout the year.

UNIQUELY BEAUTIFUL

"Courage gives us a voice, and compassion gives us an ear. Without both, there is no opportunity for empathy and connection."

—BRENÉ BROWN

Little has altered my personal view of the world more than the day I became a father. As any parent can relate, the moment you look into the eyes of your child for the very first time, everything changes. Being a dad has taught me so much about being an educator, but most of all, it's helped me truly understand the meaning of empathy. I finally understood why a mom seemed to care more about her child's happiness than her test scores at a parent meeting. I finally understood why a dad felt compelled to share insight into his son's story at a conference.

Personal and *authentic* learning isn't about an overload of data and putting a child behind a computer for the majority of a school day. It's about putting the whole child at the center of the learning experience while recognizing and valuing who that student is as an individual. *Personal* and *authentic* learning can best occur when we understand the person inside personally and the unique story that drives each learner.

For me, the importance of understanding the story inside each learner doesn't just come from my educational lens; it comes from being a dad. My little girl was born with severe food allergies—tree nuts and sesame seeds, to be exact. Not a meal goes by where we don't think about the food that's prepared, where it comes from, if it could be cross-contaminated, and any risks that could be involved. It's become a way of life, and it's something that even our extended family has become accustomed to.

When Paisley was ten months old, she accidentally ingested hummus, a food typically made with tahini—a sesame seed paste. A few minutes later, her entire body was swollen as she became almost unrecognizable, and we found ourselves rushing to the emergency room, praying to God that our baby girl was going to be okay. After a sprint through the ER and an EpiPen injection from a nurse, her tiny body began to stabilize. I had never been so scared in my life. It was that day we realized our daughter had some special needs and that certain foods would cause anaphylaxis. We were reminded how precious life is and how those we love could be gone in an instant.

I can still remember that night like it was yesterday, spending all night on the floor next to her crib, listening for each breath. I didn't sleep a wink that night and can remember just wanting to hold her close and not let go. I realized then how difficult and heart-wrenching being a parent would be at times. I didn't want my little girl to have any life struggles like this, and I will always wish there was a way I could take it from her.

Make It Stick

"Our stories are forensic evidence left by people, places, experiences, and events that touch our lives. Kids (and adults) often believe they don't have a story worth sharing because they're looking only for the big, made-for-TV moments. Our most significant stories—those that truly make us unique—are found in the microscopic, hard-to-see evidence of fingerprints of influence and impact. When we connect the dots, we find our stories; when we share our stories, we find our community."

—Brianna Hodges, educator, Texas

Four years later while having lunch away from home, Paisley took a bite of a cracker that contained sesame. For most people, it's something that they hardly notice, but for people like Paisley, this tiny seed can cause them to stop breathing. Fortunately, my five-year-old little angel instantly realized that her throat felt itchy, and she did as she has been told to do. With quick reaction time by those with her and minimal ingestion, things ended up okay—with no hospital visits or traumatic situations. The crisis had been avoided. As a parent, moments like this stop your heart and make you hold on that much tighter for the rest of the day, appreciating life's smallest moments. After hearing a story where the outcome was fatal on the news only a few days prior, I am continuously reminded how each day is a gift and how precious life really is.

After countless hugs and non-stop snuggles, we began to talk through what happened. I told Paisley how proud of her I was and how she did exactly as she was supposed to do, yet I could still see the sadness in her eyes. A little while later and while holding my hand, five-year-old Paisley looked up at me and said, "I just want to be normal, Daddy." My heart ached, and as any parent would, my eyes teared up as I held on to my little girl. A little while later, she went on to say how she wished I didn't have to worry about her, showing that her maturity and heart are far beyond her years. As a parent, these words were heart-wrenching and hard to hear, yet we remained in awe of her—how at five years old, she was able to handle a few tough cards she'd been dealt with maturity and strength. Simply put, I will always admire the courage of her little heart.

In trying to make that conversation a teachable moment, our heart-to-heart conversation led to one about appreciating all we do have and finding ways to help those who have struggles that are far more difficult than hers. As well as a five-year-old could, we talked about how everyone has some sort of struggle in life, hers being with what she eats, and how it's important to appreciate all that is right in life—understanding that many people have far more challenges than we do. I went on to tell her how her really smart brain and gorgeous smile were far from "normal" and how she is loved exactly the way she is. Her precious smile helped my heart start beating again. As hard as these conversations with someone so young and innocent may be, she was beginning to understand.

It's often been said that "the nights are long, but the years are short" when it comes to being a parent, and my wife and I have found that to be amazingly accurate. Over the next few years, we experienced incredible highs and incredible lows in life. Today, we have two amazing children, each with unique gifts and abilities, and each with their individual needs. As brother and sister, Caden and Paisley couldn't be more different, yet they are both brilliant and uniquely beautiful in their own ways.

For decades, we've talked in education about "meeting students where they are." We've spoken countless times using words such as differentiation and phrases such as "at their level." At its core, these practices have recognized the differences in those we serve. Thus, understanding that children have vastly different needs is far from a new concept; it's something that every great educator has always understood.

It's imperative to understand that making learning *personal* and *authentic* is far greater than recognizing the differences in learners. Making learning *personal* and *authentic* becomes possible when we truly understand the learner—when we understand that learner's story.

Watching my now nine-year-old girl face life with such courage has given me a new understanding of perseverance and resilience. Watching Paisley overcome her fears has challenged my views of what children are capable of and the adversity they can conquer when given the needed support along the way. It has fundamentally altered my view of what it really means to be *personal* and *authentic*.

It was in the middle of her first-grade school year that my wife, in a Facebook support group, came across "Oral Immunotherapy" (OIT), an innovative new treatment that desensitizes people to their food allergens. Having been hospitalized multiple times for the smallest levels of sesame, we were willing to try anything to help our little girl and keep her safe.

Over time, Paisley would spend forty-five days in her doctor's office undergoing therapy. For her friends, each day off from school meant time to play and relax. For Paisley, those non-school days consisted of four hours in a car and a day spent in a doctor's office outside of New York City.

During this time frame, Paisley spent one hundred and eighty hours in a car, traveling over ten thousand miles, going back and forth for her therapy. She also missed thirty-five days of school.

If someone at the school only knew the statistics or analyzed some of the data, processing thirty-five missed days of school in a year and a half, naturally, they might make some judgments. Some of them might look like this:

The parents don't care.

The family doesn't value school.

The student or parents are irresponsible.

Yet I'd guess you weren't thinking those things in this case because you understood a part of her story. You knew of her daily struggles before you could make a judgment at face value on the data.

We're often so quick to make judgments. The difference between making a judgment and having empathy is understanding the story. The stories behind the data matter—every time.

Her experience is part of her story; it's part of who she is. Her experience is not something she can leave at the front door of the school building each day.

THE DIFFERENCE BETWEEN MAKING A JUDGMENT AND HAVING EMPATHY IS UNDERSTANDING THE STORY.

Stop & REFLECT

Have you ever worked with a student who had significant medical needs? How did you ensure that student was always included? What did you learn about yourself in the process?

Just over eighteen months later, Paisley, who had been hospitalized for cross-contamination levels of sesame, would be eating the equivalent of two thousand seeds *every day*. Known as her daily "dose," what once could have taken her life is now keeping her safe.

As a dad, I'll admit that sharing such a personal story is emotional. As any parent can attest, when your child is struggling, especially with needs beyond your control, you'll do anything to take that pain and heartache from her. Besides the unparalleled support from family and friends throughout Paisley's therapy, it was the unwavering support of her teachers, Mrs. Thomas and Mr. Moyer, that carried her through.

During her year and a half of therapy, Paisley's second and third grade teachers understood that there is more to life than test scores, homework, and grades on a report card. Thank you, Mrs. Thomas and Mr. Moyer, for seeing Paisley for who she is and who she is growing to be, not as a child who regularly missed school or didn't want to be in class. Thank you for seeing her as a girl who absolutely loves school and works hard, yet at eight and then nine years old had a lot on her plate that was unrelated to academics. Thank you for going out of the way to ensure she was included, whether in the lunchroom, on a field trip, or during a classroom party. Thank you for taking care of not only her mind but also her heart. Thank you for seeing that, just like each one of her classmates, she's uniquely beautiful. Thank you for seeking to understand her hidden story.

As Paisley's dad, I will forever be in awe of the courage she showed at each doctor's visit, wondering if that would be the up-dose that put her back in the hospital. I will never forget the 566 days in a row where she would consume each night what previously could have taken her life. Although Paisley's story may be unique to her, every child and every adult that walks through our doors each day has a story that makes them who they are.

Stories of abuse.

Stories of courage.

Stories of racism.

Stories of love.

Stories of neglect.

Stories of hope.

Some of the stories that walk through our doors each day we may know well, while others remain hidden. Weaving together our experiences creates our story, makes us who we are, and determines the context in which we each learn.

Each of our stories is *personal*. Each of our stories is *authentic*. Each of our stories matters.

WEAVING TOGETHER OUR EXPERIENCES CREATES OUR STORY, MAKES US WHO WE ARE, AND DETERMINES THE CONTEXT IN WHICH WE EACH LEARN.

As educators, we must have empathy for the hidden stories within our learners and inside those with whom we work each day. Recognizing the unique beauty inside each person and the context in which they learn makes learning that is *personal* and *authentic* possible.

Stop & REFLECT

How well do you know your students? How well do you know your coworkers? How well do you know their stories? How do these stories impact how you do what you do?

Try This

> Early in the school year, ask family members to complete a questionnaire about their child, giving them opportunities to share why the student is "uniquely beautiful."

> Have family members complete an "Introducing [Student Name]" letter where they share what makes the student courageous and unique.

> On note cards, have students respond to the prompt, "I want my teacher to know . . ." at least one time per month.

> Have learners share their stories in ways they are comfortable. Celebrate differences in cultural backgrounds, religions, talents, and whatever it is that makes them proud to be unique!

A CLOSER LOOK

For a deeper dive into Chapter 3 as well as free tools, resources, and study guide questions, visit **thomascmurray.com/AuthenticEDU3.**

chapter 4

ENVISIONING PERSONAL & AUTHENTIC LEARNING EXPERIENCES

ONLY THE DREAMERS CAN ENVISION AND EXECUTE THEIR
DREAM; NO ONE ELSE CAN DO IT FOR THEM.

—KEN POIROT

Habits can be very difficult to change. Many things are so ingrained in each of our daily lives that they are almost automatic in nature. Have you ever been on your way to work and thought, "How did I get here?" having little recollection of the past number of minutes of your morning? Have you ever started a workout routine and diet on January 1, only to find yourself a few weeks later back to where you were in the months leading up to that New Year's resolution?

Habits are patterns in one's behavior and thinking. Some habits are good and beneficial to the mind and body, while others hold us back from what's possible. If our habits have more resilience than our purpose, our desired impact will be shackled.

BUILDING FOR THE FUTURE WHILE LEARNING FROM THE PAST

"The past is where you learned the lesson. The future is where you apply the lesson."

– UNKNOWN

The late Zig Ziglar, a prolific author and speaker, would often share personal stories to cause his audience members to reflect on their habits. Similar to education, in many industries, the "we've always done it that way" mindset can cause us to remain stuck in the past, blinded by our own experiences.

One story Zig would share was the time he'd won a prized country ham in a sales contest at work. Being newly married, he was so excited to bring his prize home to his new bride, Jean. He left work that afternoon, got home, and excitedly called for his wife.

Jean was so proud of her husband for winning the sales contest that she immediately decided to cook it for dinner that evening in celebration of the accomplishment. Within a few minutes, Zig could smell his winnings in the oven. He walked into the kitchen and opened the oven door to admire his prize.

"Why did you cut the end off my prized ham?" Zig called out as he opened the oven door.

"Well, that's how you bake them," Jean responded. "That's how my mama cooked a ham."

"Why did your mama do it that way?" Zig asked.

"I'm not sure," Jean responded. "Let's call mama and ask her."

Zig and Jean then called her mama, curious as to why she had always done it that way.

"Well, my mama always did it that way!" Jean's mother said.

Knowing they had to get to the bottom of this ham controversy, Zig and Jean hung up the phone and immediately called her grandmother.

"Granny," Jean began, "why do you always cut the end off the ham? Zig says I shouldn't do it that way. Mom says she cut the ham because you always cut the ham. I did it because she did it. Nobody knows why we do this. So why did you cut the end off the ham?"

"Well," said Granny, "I don't know why you two did it, but my pan was too short!"[1]

"That's the way we've always done it" are some of the most dangerous words in education. In fact, they are some of the most dangerous words in any industry.

Stop & REFLECT
What's one positive habit you have in your life? What's one habit you'd like to change? What about in your classroom or school?

Shifting our mindsets and creating new *personal* and *authentic* learning experiences for students does not mean we don't respect the incredible lessons learned from the past. There were undoubtedly amazing things happening in classrooms, even hundreds of years ago. There were also *personal* and *authentic* experiences happening in classrooms before the first computer was ever introduced. We must recognize that we often get so caught up in our own processes and traditions, we lose sight of why we used them in the first place.

The desire to change has to overcome the difficulty in doing so. Whether it's starting a new diet to alter your health, putting the phone away to be present for your family, or shifting the way we teach, breaking the chains of our ingrained actions is difficult, but it is not impossible.

THE DESIRE TO CHANGE HAS TO OVERCOME THE DIFFICULTY IN DOING SO.

In the words of Robert Frost, "The world is full of willing people—some willing to work, the rest willing to let them."[2] If we expand on Frost's thoughts and make it applicable to our world in education, we might say, "Schools are filled with willing educators—those willing to create the future and those willing to watch them do so."

Stop & REFLECT
Which type of educator are you?

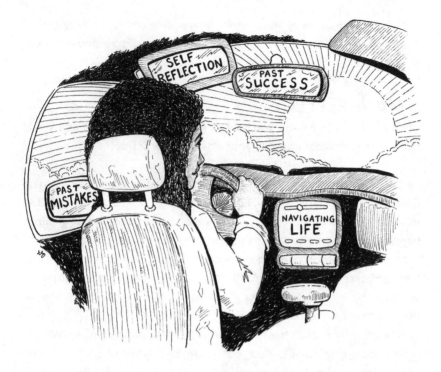

It is easy to be so hyper-focused on where we've been that we lose sight of where we are going. As we learned when we started driving, we can't accelerate and move forward if we're fixated on what's in the rearview mirror. If we attempted this, it would be our own view that blinds us. We know that the best drivers use the rearview mirror and side mirrors many times as tools throughout their journeys.

The same holds true in our schools and classrooms. Moving forward isn't about removing the rearview mirror and seeing it as unimportant. It's about using it when it's needed. We must respect and appreciate the past, as it is filled with incredible experiences for many. Today's innovations were born out of great ideas of the past; however, we must keep our nostalgia in check. Continued breakthroughs in learning sciences and technology, combined with a growing support of dynamic tools and resources, all of which we'll explore later in this book, makes what was once unthinkable in classrooms possible—and what's possible today is amazing.

How do I know? Because it's already happening. Every day, in every school, amazing *personal* and *authentic* learning experiences happen. It's time to make these types of experiences the norm and not the exception.

Try This

> Ask a colleague you respect if you can visit her classroom during instructional time to observe. Reflect on practices you feel you already do well. Seek out one or two techniques that you could learn from and ask your colleague where she learned that idea.

> Informally interview the most senior people on your staff. Ask them to reflect on the changes they've seen over time as well as the things that hold true decades later and are just as important as the day they started.

> Ask students to reflect on the best school experiences they've ever had prior to your current school year. Reflect on what those student experiences have in common and what you can learn and implement from the types of experiences they most enjoy.

VISION PROVIDES THE LIGHT

"Vision is the art of seeing what is invisible to others."
—JONATHAN SWIFT

Whether it comes at the school board level where many decisions are made regarding the future of the district, at the building level where the year has been planned, or at the classroom level related to teaching and learning, one of the most extensive needs evident in today's schools is a clear vision of the path forward. A lack of vision is often to blame for the feeling of one spinning their wheels or the cause of a large state of confusion. Being able to see the finish line makes running the race plausible, and it makes the end goal attainable.

It's been said that the fewest number of people quit running a marathon during the first mile. Barring any injury, almost all people who have signed up to run a marathon know they can conquer the first mile of the race, as it's something they've done consistently, often as the simple warm-up for their extensive training. Having just begun the race, one's durability is strong, energy levels are high, and confidence levels are pure. Common sense would think that over the course of the race, those who stop running and quit the race would increase with each passing mile. Why? With each passing step, more energy is burned, muscles tighten, the risk of injury increases, and the mental exhaustion escalates.

Surprisingly, though, this isn't the case. Statistically, the second fewest number of people quit the race in the final mile. One might expect the largest number of runners to quit in the last mile after the most amount of energy has been burned, and the body has hit peak levels of exhaustion. Why isn't this the case?

As runners hit that twenty-sixth mile, they can physically see, or at least visualize, the finish line. Although the journey has been excruciating, the vision is about to be realized. Although the body says, "Stop!" the mind says, "Keep going, I can see the finish line! I'm almost there!" A prime example of this level of determination occurred during the 2015 Austin (Texas) Marathon.

Lifelong Kenyan runner Hyvon Ngetich led the competition for most of the race. In the final mile, she started to suffer from dangerously low blood sugar, and, with only two-tenths of a mile remaining, became unbalanced and fell to the ground. With the finish line in sight and those around her cheering her on, Ngetich never stopped moving forward. Giving all that she had, this champion from Kenya crawled on the pavement for the final 400 meters to finish the race. With the end goal in sight, Ngetich dragged herself to finish what she had started just over three hours prior.[3]

Without the vision of the goal being attainable, Ngetich may not have had the courage to persevere and finish the race. It was her vision of attaining what she set out to do that made overcoming all the obstacles possible.

Contrasting Ngetich's heroic display, most runners who walk away from and quit their marathon before the finish line do so around the twentieth mile. At this point in the race, the body has little left to give, the runner has given their all, the pain seems insurmountable, and the end goal is not yet in sight. Without the vision of achieving what they had long trained for, the struggles of the body can more easily overcome the power of the mind.

Stop & REFLECT

What's your marathon example? What race are you struggling to run? Do you have a clear vision for what you're working to attain?

"Everybody ends up somewhere in life. A few people end up somewhere on purpose."
—ANDY STANLEY

Today, some of you are feeling like the end goal is not in sight. Some of you are feeling like you're spinning your wheels month after month. Some of you may even feel as if you are running the twentieth mile, have nothing left, and are crawling on the proverbial pavement, just trying to survive. Without a vision of what you're running to, giving up can seem like a strong possibility.

It is difficult to change oneself and one's habits and behaviors. Change only becomes possible when a path forward is visible and understood. It is the vision of the desired outcomes that provides the light to make attaining the end goal possible.

Every invention began with a vision of something that didn't yet exist.

Every act of immense courage during the civil rights era began with a vision of equality.

Every Super-Bowl-winning season began with a vision of hoisting the Lombardi Trophy.

Every school transformation begins with a vision of what could be—a "North Star" of purpose.

During ancient times, when caravans would navigate unknown territories, routes were plotted by locating the North Star. With about five thousand stars visible on a clear night, why did this particular star have such significance?

Amid a chaotic sky, filled with thousands of possible stars that could be used as a natural compass, the North Star, also known as Polaris, appears to remain unmoved in the midst of a rotating star field. In the vast, seemingly unending sky above, the North Star identifies the sky's north pole because it is the location around which the entire sky turns. As the world turns in circles, the North Star remains stable and unchanged.

Every educator has an innate desire to do something amazing and to be part of something great. Every employee in a school—whether bearing the title of principal, teacher, or support staff member—has the desire to create learning experiences in which students thrive. The desire is there, but many times the vision for how to get there is missing.

Creating *personal* and *authentic* learning experiences in schools can only happen when a clear vision for the teaching and learning is present and understood. Teachers and administrators can't do what they don't know is possible. Students can't become what they don't know exists.

So what's your vision to create learner-centered experiences that are *personal* and *authentic* in nature? Where do such experiences already exist in your classroom or school? What do these experiences look like? What characteristics make them relevant to the learners?

As we move forward on our journey, it's important to remember that the road to success doesn't always lie straight ahead. There will be twists and turns and even potholes along the way. Remember Noah's ark was built by first-timers but was successful because the builders had the ultimate vision, passion, and purpose in the work that needed to be done.

WITH A CLEAR VISION FOR WHAT YOU'RE GOING TO CREATE FOR YOUR STUDENTS, IT IS YOUR PASSION THAT WILL FUEL YOUR ABILITY TO FOLLOW THROUGH AND SUSTAIN YOUR ULTIMATE PURPOSE.

Creating *personal* and *authentic* learning experiences for learners must be part of our North Star. With a clear vision for what you're going to create for your students, it is your passion that will fuel your ability to follow through and sustain your ultimate purpose.

IN PRACTICE

JUSTIN AGLIO, EdD, DIRECTOR OF
ACADEMIC ACHIEVEMENT AND DISTRICT
INNOVATION, MONTOUR SCHOOL
DISTRICT, PENNSYLVANIA

Putting Children First, Supporting a Growth Mindset, and *Creating a Learning Culture* serve as the unwavering core values of the Montour School District. Montour uses these three core values to align its priorities in order to provide a kid-centered, future-focused learning culture.

Decisions at all levels within the district, from a macro to a micro level, align to Montour's core values. The core values serve as an authentic resource that is used as the framework when developing curriculum, creating learning opportunities, evaluating resources, and assessing partnerships. Furthermore, the core values at Montour enable a systemic approach of a unified voice that complements the individual talents of students and team members at Montour.

One example of Montour's core values is its vision and approach in creating a robust and relevant STEM program. Students are encouraged to be curious and learn skills and strategies that promote self-agents of change. The STEM program supports students' interests by creating meaningful learning experiences, such as the world's first brick makerspace powered by LEGO Education Solutions and Minecraft Lab. In addition, an artificial intelligence (AI) program was created through a series of courses developed and implemented by Montour team members and partners. The goal for the program is to make an all-inclusive AI program for students in a world where children live and to prepare them for a future where they will thrive.

Overall, the strength of Montour's core values is not in the words but in who developed the core values—the people of Montour. Montour believes that innovation starts and ends *with people.* The quality of the services provided to all stakeholders at Montour are due to the authenticity of the core values that were genuinely crafted and implemented *by people* and *for people.* Although educators at Montour cannot predict the future, Montour strives for continual improvement and believes the core values at Montour will help design the future that educators envision to optimize learning.

Try This

> Fold a large sheet of paper into thirds horizontally. On the left section, identify five to ten skills or characteristics you want your students to have one year from today. In the center section, identify three to four ways in which you currently help cultivate each one of those skills. On the right-hand section, identify two to three ways you can further build each skill in your curricular area(s).

> Elementary: Ask students to design and create a passion project around the theme "One problem I'd like to solve in the future . . ."

> Secondary: Have students write about or video produce, using the theme "The person I want to be in five years . . ."

> Work diligently with students to help develop their success pathways to help them prepare for their post-graduation goals, allowing for maximum flexibility along the way.

DEVELOPING A LEARNER-CENTERED PARADIGM

"You can't mandate learning, but you can create the conditions where people are inspired and empowered to learn."

—KATIE MARTIN

Take a moment to think back to your high school experience. What classes were your favorites? What experiences did you enjoy most? During which experiences did you learn the most? Who's the first teacher that you think of from your experience? Why?

The notion of being "learner-centered" isn't new. Since the one-room schoolhouse, the best teachers recognized learners as individuals with unique interests, passions, and talents. Since the very first schools, the best teachers have recognized the need to include the heart when trying to grow the mind. Since the first schools, the best teachers knew that the learners were the purpose of the work. It's no doubt that education is the greatest investment one can make in oneself and in others. The ability to obtain an education is the foundation of every democracy. An educated society enables progress and solves world problems. Although the value of education has long been understood, understanding the science of learning and how learning actually occurs has been limited in the past.

If we are learner-centered, it means that we, as educators, have to evolve as the world does. With advances in technology in areas such as artificial intelligence and predictive analytics and the research being done in the field of learning sciences, our practices, tools, and environments will shift, but our focus on the learners and how to support them to reach their full potential remains the goal. Fortunately, in recent years, breakthroughs in these "learning sciences" have escalated and focus on the why, the what, and the how of learning, both in and out of school.

To be learner-centered, we have to understand how learners actually learn best. The more we understand how people learn, the more we can understand how to create more *personal* and *authentic* experiences.

Researchers and educators alike know that what an individual learns is a function of cultural, social, and environmental constructs. Yet for years, neuroscientists and educators did their work in complete silos. More recently, however, the teaming of those who study how the brain works with those who work with children every day has provided significant understanding as to how to best create learner-centered *personal* and *authentic* experiences. Today, places such as Johns Hopkins University and organizations such as the Alliance for Excellent Education and Digital Promise are working to mold the two areas to improve student learning experiences.

Research in neuroscience has indicated that learning occurs in three main phases:[4]

1. **Encoding:** Transforming experiences into long-term memory
2. **Storage:** Storing the experience and information over time
3. **Retrieval:** Accessing the experience and information on demand

Any educator or researcher will agree that learning is a complex process filled with many variables. From the spaces in which kids learn to their emotional well-being, learning goes far deeper than consuming information that's presented. So what is currently known about how to best be learner-centered? What can we understand from advances in neuroscience to help us provide more *personal* and *authentic* experiences for our learners?

Digital Promise (digitalpromise.org), an educational non-profit organization, and the Institute for Applied Neuroscience (appliedneuro.org) synthesized the findings from research on the learning sciences and developed the following "10 Key Principles" of how people learn, along with practical suggestions as to how these understandings correlate to educational practice.[5]

THE LEARNING SCIENCES: 10 KEY PRINCIPLES

1. Learning is a process that involves effort, mistakes, reflection, and a refinement of strategies.
2. Thinking deeply about the to-be-learned material helps students pay attention, build memories, and make meaning out of what they are learning.
3. Communicating high expectations and keeping learners at the edge of their mastery helps students reach their potential.
4. Retrieval practice strengthens memory and helps students flexibly apply what they learn.
5. Spacing out learning and interweaving different content strengthens learning.
6. Students are more motivated to learn when they are interested, have a sense of autonomy, and understand the purpose behind what they are learning.
7. Students learn well when they feel safe and connected.
8. Collaboration and social interaction can be powerful learning

experiences because they encourage deeper processing and engage the "social brain."

9. Students' physical well-being, including nutrition, sleep, and exercise, impacts learning.

10. The entire environment, from space to temperature to lighting, can affect learning.

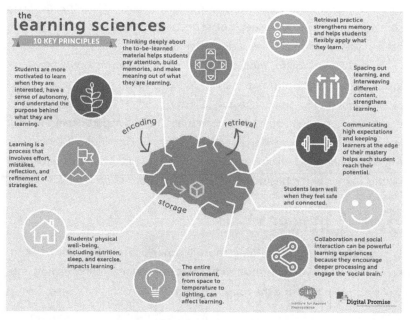

Image Credit: Courtesy of Digital Promise

You'll notice a significant overlap between the "10 Key Principles" and the content throughout this book. Why? It's imperative that, as we proceed with changes to protocol and pedagogy, our decision-making remains evidence-based.

Stop & REFLECT

Which principle resonates with you the most? Why? Which principles correlate with what you've read so far in this book? What's one principle you could focus on more in your work?

Our students are not guinea pigs. They are not test mice in an experimentation lab. They are learners filled with interests, passions, talents, and a world of potential. They need and deserve experiences that are grounded in effective practices and the knowledge we have about how the brain functions. We must separate what sounds good from what actually works.

Creating *personal* and *authentic* experiences happens inside a learner-centered paradigm. This shift in thinking is similar to what happens when someone gets a new pair of glasses. These lenses offer a new focus, a new way to envision, process, and implement learning experiences. This shift puts the learner at the heart of all decision-making and builds the necessary systems of support around each individual.

In such a paradigm, individuals are seen as *learners*, which entails growth and agency, and not merely *students*, which has sometimes correlated with more compliance and less control. In learner-centered paradigms, learners are respected as individuals, are active participants in their learning, and gain ownership over the process by developing agency over time. *Personal* and *authentic* learning thrives in paradigms that are focused on the learner, and it begins with the very first impression.

Stop & REFLECT

Is your classroom or building more learner-centered or teacher-centered? How can you continue to take steps forward, relinquishing control over time, to refine the focus on your learners?

Try This

> Choose one of the "10 Key Principles" each week for ten weeks. Find ways to discuss with both students and colleagues their thoughts on what aspects of the brain-based principle are currently in place and ways in which it could be improved.

> Leverage student interest inventories to get to know their likes, dislikes, and passion areas.

> Ask five students for feedback on something you could do to make the learning space more learner-centered. Implement at least two of their ideas.

> Identify the last few learning experiences you've led. Analyze what choice and ownership students had throughout the process.

> Ensure students set goals as part of the learning process. Empower them to set the desired outcomes, track their growth, obtain the needed resources, and celebrate in their successes.

> Read and reflect on *Learner-Centered Innovation: Spark Curiosity, Ignite Passion and Unleash Genius* by Katie Martin.

Make It Stick

"Leverage social media to connect with your families. Reading a bedtime story using Facebook Live on the night before the first day of school helps new students put a face with a name. For returning students, it helps them remember the smiling face who will be welcoming them in the morning. For parents, it reminds them we care about their most prized possession and are excited to welcome their child back for another fabulous year of learning and growing together."

—Tara Desiderio, elementary school principal, Pennsylvania

INTENTIONAL FIRST IMPRESSIONS

"You never get a second chance to make a first impression."
— UNKNOWN

The first interaction with the person that became your best friend. Your last first date. The first moments after becoming a parent. The first moments of a job interview. The first day of school. Life is filled with first impressions—and, scientifically, they have an impact.

Recall the most recent first impression you've had. How did the impression alter the rest of your experience?

In his book *WHEN: The Scientific Secrets of Perfect Timing*, Daniel Pink highlights the importance of when things happen. Pink utilizes research behind beginnings, midpoints, and endings and shows how vital each one is, from relationships to life experiences. He also points to a direct overlap of our work as educators and the importance of the first impressions that we make. How teachers begin the school year or the first impressions they have on their students in the classroom were examples that resonated with me.

If we are going to make learning experiences *personal* and *authentic* for students, we must be intentional about the first impressions we make.

I often think back to my first day as a teacher. Twenty-one years old and fresh out of college, I did exactly what I had experienced as a student because it was what I knew. My first day of teaching was filled with passing out every textbook and folder that my students would use, assigning classroom numbers, filling out index cards full of information, and extensively reviewing "Mr. Murray's Classroom Rules."

Seven hours later, the students left with backpacks full of materials for the year, a list of textbooks to be covered that evening, information they had to retrieve from their parents, and an earful of expectations for that upcoming year.

Sound familiar?

What a missed opportunity. There's no chance that my kids went home thinking, "I can't wait to do that again tomorrow!"

So much of my first day of teaching was about me when it could have been about them. Under the guidance of tremendous mentors, I vastly altered that first day in my second year and every year after that. We moved from starting the year with a culture of compliance to a culture of innovation and fun. We'd spend the first few days building the team, creating our collaborative expectations, and highlighting some of the most dynamic learning experiences we would have together that year.

In reflecting on my own experiences, from my vast failures to our many team successes, I encourage teachers and principals to consider the following questions any time they have the incredible opportunity to serve a new set of students. I do so not to pretend that I had it all together in the classroom or had any of these mastered when I taught or was a principal, as I certainly didn't. I pose these questions to help create the types of *personal* and *authentic* learning experiences our students need and deserve—and to kick it all off with memorable first impressions.

1. What will you do on day one that will have your kids running back to your classroom on day two?

When I reflect on what I just shared about my very first day teaching, I can't imagine that my students went home on day one inspired to come back on day two. Fortunately, after focusing the first few days of year two on relationship and culture building, day one became something we all enjoyed. What a difference a year made for my students and for me.

If you're the chemistry teacher, why not start blowing things up on day one? (Then, of course, make a connection between the explosion to the chemical reactions you'll be studying that year.) If you're the biology teacher, why not start day one with a dissection? If you teach fourth grade, why not take the first few hours together to be outside doing team-building activities and spend the rest of the day doing hands-on activities, previewing some of the most authentic experiences they'll have that year?

Why not? We can. In fact, many do.

When your kids get home from the first day of school, at what point will they stop talking about what they did that day? What will they share when they get home? Simply put, spending day one on logistics, rules, and book covers won't have them running back to you on day two, nor will it give them much to talk about when they get home. Building relationships and creating *personal* and *authentic* experiences, however, will.

2. If students saw your classroom design before the first day of school, what types of learning experiences would they expect?

My first day of teaching started with desks in rows, my large
teacher's desk up front, and a
room setup that led to me standing up front to disseminate information. The classroom layout
indicated that I would be transferring the knowledge to the students as they sat, desks in rows,
islands unto themselves, ready
to obtain all that I would share.

Make It Stick

"Create a vision board with your
students using images and words that
represent hopes and goals for the new
school year to set positive intentions
and focus for the new year."

—Akela Silkman, instructional
technology specialist, Virginia

Learning space design, a topic discussed in Chapter 6, has a profound impact on the way students learn. Research indicates that design
can empower or hinder learning. What research are you using to design
your classroom or school space? Ultimately, what does the learning space
design indicate about your beliefs regarding how effective teaching and
learning occurs? Does the classroom design give the impression that it will
be more about you or more about them?

3. How will you intentionally build relationships with and among your students?

What if you took the first few days of school or a new semester to focus
on building culture and relationships? What if the first few days were filled
with team-building experiences? What if the first few days were spent previewing some of the best experiences your learners will have during their
time with you? How would such a mindset then impact your relationships
with them?

What's fascinating to me is that the more we focus on a "testing culture," which raises the "we don't have time for . . ." mantra, the less we as
educators feel we can do to build relationships and culture in our classrooms. I fully understand where this mindset comes from and that quite
often poor leadership in a school reinforces and prioritizes these expectations. This notion, however, is entirely counterintuitive to learning science
research and all we know about effective teaching and learning. Without a
personal and *authentic* relationship, it is nearly impossible to create deeper
learning experiences.

Although I may not have created the best first impressions that first
year, countless educators do an incredible job setting the tone for the

time together and getting learners excited about what's to come. From the moment that first bell rings, these educators create environments where kids want to be and ultimately remain the center of it all throughout the year.

Creating these *personal* and *authentic* first impressions is in no way the sole responsibility of the teachers in a building, as principals must model the way. Having learned from so many mentors early in my career, I had one principal mentor in particular who understood the importance of first impressions and the power of what can be done in the time leading up to the first day of school. Thank you to Deb Lock for the following idea.

Not only does the first impression of kindergarten indicate what the year will hold, but it also gives a first impression of a child's school career. Continuing the tradition from the elementary school principal who preceded me, each summer I'd invite our core team—school counselor, reading specialist, and instructional support teacher—to our "Summer Kindergarten Doorstep Visits" that we shared we'd be doing with parents in the summer mailing. Beginning school at the end of August in the northeast, we'd spend a week and a half in the late summer visiting every kindergarten student at the doorstep of his home. We'd bring school pride swag and a copy of the book *First Day Jitters* for each child to welcome them to our school community. After spending a few minutes there, we'd personally invite the children and their families to our kindergarten orientation at the end of the month, and before we left, we'd get down to eye level with the children to let them know how excited we were that they were joining our school family. A week before kindergarten orientation, we'd mail out a handwritten note to each child, telling them how great it was to meet them and how we were so excited to see them again at orientation in a few days.

Did over fifty home visits and handwritten notes take an extreme amount of time each year? Absolutely. Was it worth it to show our kids and their families how much they mattered to us? Without a doubt. When the children came to their very first day of school, they were met by adults who had been to their homes, had previously met one of their family members, and had written them personal notes to show them how much they mattered.

First impressions matter. It's why we must be *intentional* about them.

Whether it's the principal that leverages Facebook Live to read to students before the first night of school, the teacher that uses Flipgrid to record words of encouragement from parents to share with students on the first day, or the "Tunnel of Kindness" created by high school staff members as the students reenter for the new year, creating *personal* and *authentic* learner-centered experiences begins with the first impression.

Stop & REFLECT

What can you do for your next group of students that will give them a first impression they and their families will remember for years to come?

Try This

> Before the first day of school, call each family and share how excited you are to have their child in your class that year.

> On the first day, bring a bag full of items that represent who you are and what you enjoy doing. On day two, have students do the same. Give each student the opportunity to share, just like you did on day one.

Make It Stick

"On the first day, give each student a different jelly bean to eat. Ask them to describe what they taste, and words like yuck, sweet, terrible, and really good will likely be mentioned. Explain to them that the different taste experiences are a metaphor for the moments they had before your class, and although they are now gone, they can still be remembered, and this year is a fresh start. Then give them a small bag with a jelly bean to keep in their locker for the rest of the year to remember the good things, while letting go of the not-so-good things."

—Shawn Storm, middle school teacher, Pennsylvania

> Before sharing your expectations with students, ask them their expectations of you.

> Play "Two Truths and a Lie" as a fun, interactive way for the new classroom community to get to know one another.

> Instead of covering books on the first night of school, have students share their first day with their parents what they are most excited about and their goals for the year.

> Recruit a greeter! Can you partner with a senior center to have a greeter who welcomes each child with a smile every morning?

> At the end of the year, have students write a letter to next year's students about what they loved most about your class. Use these letters over the summer or on the first day back to pique students' interest about what's to come.

Elementary

> Prior to the first day of school, ask the previous year's teachers to identify the "best characteristic" of each of your students. Then send a handwritten note, addressed to the student, welcoming him to the class, sharing what you've already heard, and that you're excited to meet him.

> Study the names and faces of your students prior to day one. As they enter the classroom for the first time, greet each student at the door by name.

Secondary

> On the first day of school, preview two or three of the best learning experiences that students will have during their time with you that year.

> As students enter the classroom on first day back, roll out the red carpet and give them the royal treatment to kick things off.

A CLOSER LOOK

For a deeper dive into Chapter 4 as well as free tools, resources, and study guide questions, visit **thomascmurray.com/AuthenticEDU4**.

chapter 5

DESIGNING PERSONAL & AUTHENTIC LEARNING EXPERIENCES

THE QUESTION THAT MUST BE ASKED EVERY DAY IS, 'WHAT IS BEST FOR THIS LEARNER?'

—GEORGE COUROS

ohnny, president of the National Honor Society and ranked at the top of his graduating class, received scholarship offers from a large number of universities. His high SAT scores, combined with his 4.0 GPA, enabled him to choose where he wanted to go to school the following year. Having taken five advanced placement (AP) courses during his senior year, he also earned top scores on his AP exams, so he would be transferring college credits to the next level. The hometown newspaper headline read, "School District's Top Student is Ready for Success!"

Johnny's fictional example would be deemed quite the school district success story, right?

Every school district has graduates just like Johnny. Do you know what else many school districts have each year? Graduates just like Johnny with all the possible academic accolades and a heart that is crumbling. Graduates just like Johnny who struggle with anxiety and depression. Graduates just like Johnny who struggle with their own self-worth. In the worst possible cases, in some places, graduates just like Johnny who take their own lives shortly after high school graduation. If we care more about a child's academic accolades than we do about his or her heart, we have completely lost our way.

IF WE CARE MORE ABOUT A CHILD'S ACADEMIC ACCOLADES THAN WE DO ABOUT HIS OR HER HEART, WE HAVE COMPLETELY LOST OUR WAY.

THE SOCIAL-EMOTIONAL SIDE MAKES LEARNING POSSIBLE

"There is abundant evidence that when districts and schools explicitly and meaningfully commit to focusing on the students' comprehensive development as a central part of their academic growth, the academic success and the welfare of students rise powerfully together."

—A NATION AT HOPE

Students can graduate with the highest academic honors, high SAT scores, and high GPAs, but if our focus is solely on academic data and not on the individual as a whole, we have failed them. We may have prepared them with academic skills, but we have failed to prepare them for life. Today, seven in ten teens think anxiety and depression are major problems for their peers, six in ten feel pressure to get good grades, and three in ten feel pressure to look good and fit in socially.[1]

Make It Stick

"Have students write friendly letters to you early in the school year, sharing about who they are and what they enjoy. Then write an intentional and personal note back to each student to show how you value each one of them."

—Ryan McHale, middle school teacher, Massachusetts

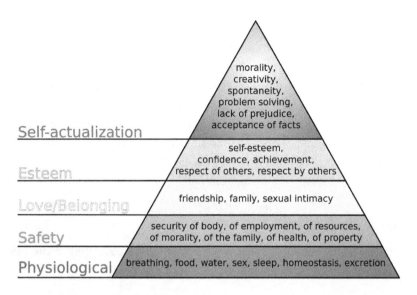

Learning that is *personal* and *authentic* puts Maslow before Bloom every day of the week. It values more than academics. I also believe those who view learners solely as data points and assessment scores can do more harm than good.

This is why the greatest teachers are far more than content deliverers. It is why the best principals care far more about their students as individuals than they do about their building's test scores. It is why the most effective educators create places where learners *want to be*, not simply places they have to be. Caring about the social-emotional side of learning isn't just a nice thing to do; it's the only way to live. There is great synergy between a child's well-being and his or her ability to learn.

THERE IS GREAT SYNERGY BETWEEN A CHILD'S WELL-BEING AND HIS OR HER ABILITY TO LEARN.

During their schooling, virtually every educator has studied "Maslow's Hierarchy of Needs," a theory in psychology developed by Abraham Maslow in his 1943 paper, "A Theory of Human Motivation."[2] Maslow's theory parallels many other human development theories, as it describes the stages of human needs and growth. Used to study how humans will intrinsically take part in behavioral motivation, Maslow's original hierarchy included

"Physiological," "Safety," "Belonging and Love," "Social Needs," "Esteem," and "Self-Actualization" to describe the five-tier model of human needs and is often visualized as levels within a pyramid structure.[3] In his theory, human needs lower on the pyramid must be satisfied before individuals are able to attain higher levels of esteem and self-actualization; for example, individuals lacking the basic necessities of life, such as food, water, and sleep (physiological), will struggle to be able to concern themselves with problem-solving and creativity (self-actualization).

Sound relevant for our today's learners?

Stop & REFLECT

Think of students you've had who struggled because their basic life needs weren't being met. How did you support them?

We don't need a long-standing psychological theory to understand the imperative need for the social-emotional side to learning. Any educator can verify from personal experience that a student's well-being is a natural ally to his or her ability to learn at deep levels.

If you found yourself nodding your head and agreeing with what you just read, what are you doing about it? As a teacher, how do you make sure you connect with the heart and not just the mind? As a principal, how do you prioritize the well-being of students above academic needs? What do you do to support the whole child?

At Cold Springs Middle School in Nevada, teachers intentionally collaborate to ensure the well-being of every one of the almost one thousand children who walk through the doors of their middle school. Social-emotional learning (SEL) in this school isn't about a handful of lessons or putting on a smile in the hallway. It's about intentionally ensuring they are active in seeking support, making connections, and monitoring the needs of *every child* they serve.

Started by Principal Roberta Duvall at this rural middle school outside of Reno, staff members come together to review the school roster on posters around the room, using colored markers to make check marks under columns labeled "Name/Face," "Something Personal," "Personal/Family Story," and "Academic Standing" to indicate if they know the children by name, by face, their personal stories, and how they are performing in the classroom.

Staff members review every child in the school and cross-reference information with their colleagues. What has become a foundational practice in this Nevada middle school also visually indicates which students have personal connections and which students are only known by name or face. Early on, it was evident that some kids had check marks in all categories. What also became apparent was that some kids had minimal connections to the adults in the building, and their world outside of school was a mystery to all staff members.

Being intentional about SEL has pushed staff members to look beyond their lessons and reflect on how well they know the students they teach and those who walk the halls of the school each day.

Cold Spring Middle School is part of the 64,000-student Washoe County School District in Nevada. In 2012, the district, comprised of ninety-eight schools, launched a comprehensive SEL program, as it understood how social and emotional skills such as perseverance and empathy can help improve student success in many areas. The district also adopted the mission statement, "Every Child, by Name and Face, to Graduation."

Since implementing an SEL-based approach to their work, Washoe School District has seen attendance rates increase and had fewer discipline issues while earning higher state test scores and seeing more profound social-emotional skills in place. Since prioritizing cultures where students were valued for far more than their academics, graduation rates increased eighteen points across the district in the program's first five years.[4]

Prioritizing the social-emotional aspects of learning helps us see more than what we teach. It helps us see who we teach.

Being *personal* and *authentic* means recognizing the needs of each individual and not merely considering the overall well-being of the group. There is no area where this is more evident than in today's mental health crisis.

PRIORITIZING THE SOCIAL-EMOTIONAL ASPECTS OF LEARNING HELPS US SEE MORE THAN WHAT WE TEACH. IT HELPS US SEE WHO WE TEACH.

According to the National Alliance on Mental Illness:[5]

> "Approximately 1 in 5 adults in the U.S.—43.8 million, or 18.5%—experiences mental illness in a given year.

> Approximately 1 in 5 youth aged 13–18 (21.4%) experiences a severe mental disorder at some point during their life. For children aged 8–15, the estimate is 13%.

> Over one-third (37%) of students with a mental health condition aged 14–21 and older who are served by special education drop out—the highest dropout rate of any disability group."

According to the Centers for Disease Control and Prevention (September 2017):

> "Suicide is the third leading cause of death for youth between the ages of 10 and 24.

> A nationwide survey of high school students in the U.S. found that 16% of students reported seriously considering suicide, 13% reported creating a plan, and 8% reported trying to take their own lives in the 12 months preceding the survey.

> Each year, approximately 157,000 youth between the ages of 10 and 24 are treated in U.S. Emergency Departments for self-inflicted injuries."

Although these numbers represent statistics from the United States only, these issues are prevalent around the world. One of the challenges of being an educator today is that we are often put in positions of being asked to help fix large-scale societal issues. From feeding and clothing students who live in poverty to guiding those who struggle with mental health, educators find themselves trying to do it all.

What's amazing is that educators find a way to do it all. Serving those in need is ingrained in who they are. It's part of the reason why educators are some of the most talented, empathetic, incredible people on the planet.

Stop & REFLECT

What child is on your heart right now? What child does the above section remind you of? What structures of support are in place for that child?

In traditional settings, SEL is often viewed as the responsibility of a few staff members, such as a school counselor or district psychologist, and reserved for those students who require treatment or documented levels of support. Today's best schools and districts recognize the responsibility of *all staff members* to prioritize the social-emotional needs of students while intentionally creating structures of support. Districts that want to increase student achievement should start by increasing support for SEL.

From a Nation at Risk to a Nation at Hope, a report from the National Commission on Social, Emotional, and Academic Development, summarized our work as educators and the importance of SEL:

> *Children require a broad array of skills, attitudes, and values to succeed in school, careers, and in life. They require skills such as paying attention, setting goals, collaboration, and planning for the future. They require attitudes such as internal motivation, perseverance, and a sense of purpose. They require values such as responsibility, honesty, and integrity. They require the abilities to think critically, consider different views, and problem-solve. And these social, emotional, and academic capacities are increasingly demanded in the American workplace, which puts a premium on the ability to work in diverse teams, to grapple with difficult problems, and to adjust to rapid change.*
>
> *Helping children to learn these traits and skills may sound ambitious. But it is—and has always been—central to the educational enterprise. It is the reason that education begins with concerned and involved*

Make It Stick

"Educators have the potential to have a lifelong impact on a student's trajectory in life. The whole child approach teaches students about perseverance and resilience, two essential skills every student will need at some point in life to be successful."

—Basil Marin, high school assistant principal, Georgia

parents, who provide emotional support and set high expectations. It is the reason that community institutions that mentor children and encourage self-respect are essential allies of parents and schools. It is the reason that good teachers can change lives, helping students find unsuspected gifts and inner purpose. And it is the reason that everyone involved in education shares an amazing calling: to foster in children the knowledge, skills, and character that enable children to make better lives in a better country.

This calling is an honor, but not an elective. Since all education involves social, emotional, and academic learning, we have but two choices: We can either ignore that fact and accept disappointing results or address these needs intentionally and well.[7]

SEL is not some educational fad, an add-on to a single lesson, or a pre-purchased, canned curriculum. It's at the core of all the work we do as educators.

You don't teach math. *You teach kids math.*

You don't teach science. *You teach kids science.*

You don't teach music. *You teach kids music.*

You don't teach social studies. *You teach kids social studies.*

You don't teach writing. *You teach kids writing.*

Some view the difference in syntax above as a nuance. Others see this nuance as the purpose of their work.

Learning that is *personal* and *authentic* can only happen when children are treated as human beings, with their social, emotional, and academic needs all valued. If we are to push a child's mind, we must utilize the lever that starts at the heart. The "how" of *personal* and *authentic* learning in the classroom begins here.

IF WE ARE TO PUSH A CHILD'S MIND, WE MUST UTILIZE THE LEVER THAT STARTS AT THE HEART.

Try This

> Choose your students' favorite emojis to highlight how they might be feeling on a given day. Consolidate these onto a feedback form, either on paper or digitally, and use them as intro or exit slips to gauge how they are feeling when they enter the classroom or how they felt about a lesson, allowing it to be used for both SEL and instructional purposes.

> Be vulnerable in the work and show your human side, not just all that you know.

> When you see a child struggling emotionally, make it your mission to get them the help they need, and do everything in your power to show them how valued they are.

> Therapy dogs are becoming very common in schools and showing promise in supporting the social-emotional side to learning. Could your school adopt one?

CULTURALLY RESPONSIVE

"Culturally responsive teaching is about helping culturally and linguistically diverse students who have been marginalized in schools build their skill and capacity to do rigorous work. The focus isn't on motivation but on improving their brainpower and information processing skills."

— ZARETTA HAMMOND

According to the Pew Research Center (2018),[8] "post-millennials" (also referred to as "Generation Z" or "the iGen"), those born between 1997 and 2012, are on track to be the "most diverse and best-educated generation yet." An increase in diverse backgrounds, combined with higher high school graduation rates, shows incredible promise for today's generation of learners. Although statistics are different for each country, in the United States, student demographics have evolved to the following:

> 52% are non-Latinx white

> 25% are Latinx

> 14% are Black

> 6% are Asian

> <4% are non-Latinx of another racial identity, mainly two or more races

A longitudinal review of the demographic composite in the United States shows a long-term trend in an increasingly diverse population, undoubtedly a strength for the nation's future.

Generation[9]	% of 6–21-year-olds who are non-white
Post-Millennials in 2018	48%
Millennials in 2002	39%
Gen Xers in 1986	30%
Early Boomers in 1968	18%

As educators, we have the moral and ethical obligation to ensure that the work we do respects, appreciates, and values diversity and diverse perspectives. If we are going to create *personal* and *authentic* learning experiences, being culturally responsive is a non-negotiable. Children can't learn where they aren't valued and respected. Inclusive environments, for students and staff alike, are imperative.

As a white male, it is my obligation to ensure that other white educators understand the need for culturally responsive experiences. I simultaneously recognize that my lens isn't the one that should be leading this conversation, as so many educators have far more and

Make It Stick

"As teachers and librarians, we must develop inclusive collections that include and celebrate the voices, ideas, and experiences of all people in our society. These materials need to represent current and historical issues and points of views, ensuring that everyone is represented and heard. And always remembering, one of the most important factors in developing our collections is involving our young people in this process and including windows and doors into their world."

—Shannon Miller, librarian, Iowa

vastly different experiences than I do and need to be heard. Thus, it's an honor to amplify the voice of my amazing friend, Dr. Rosa Perez-Isiah for the rest of this section.

CULTURALLY RESPONSIVE TEACHING IS THE ONLY WAY

-DR. ROSA PEREZ-ISIAH, DIRECTOR, ELEMENTARY, CALIFORNIA

Early in my educational career, I discovered that *culturally responsive* teaching and leading are *non-negotiables* in education. Looking back, culturally responsive teachers addressed my needs as an English learner and student of color, and later in life, it was who I grew to be as a young educator of diverse student populations. When I had an opportunity to lead, it was part of what others referred to as my "leadership style." But I repeatedly wondered . . .

Isn't this the way we should all teach, lead, and learn?

Should we not view education through a culturally responsive lens?

How could we possibly teach without addressing, validating, uplifting, and learning from the diverse beings in our schools and classrooms?

Our students come to us with an abundance of assets and experiences. These experiences are part of who they are and greatly impact their identities as scholars. Unfortunately, those rich experiences have been ignored, dismissed, or perceived to be deficits by our educational system for too long. Educators are failing to view those experiences as assets and failing to tap into the funds of knowledge possessed by our students. Language, culture, ethnicity, color, gender, lived experiences . . . all of these factors contribute to our learning and how we function as human beings. When those *funds of knowledge* are recognized and culturally responsive, teaching becomes more than a professional development topic in the schoolhouse; true learning can transpire for all children.

Jacqueline J. Irvine and Willis D. Hawley conducted an overview of research on Culturally Responsive Pedagogy titled *Culturally Responsive Pedagogy: An Overview of Research on Student Outcomes* (2011). They shared the following about the importance and characteristics of a Culturally Responsive Teacher:

> "Culturally responsive teachers understand that students bring their culturally influenced cognition, behavior, and dispositions with them to school. These teachers not only understand student differences related to race, ethnicity, culture, and language, but they use this knowledge to enrich their teaching in ways that enhance learning opportunities. Achievement relevant student assets, according to Hurley, Allen, and Boykin (2009), include students' interests and preferences; motivational inclinations; passions and commitments; prior experiences and knowledge; existent and emergent understandings and skills; personal, family, and cultural values; family traditions and practices; attitudes, beliefs, and opinions; self-perceptions; and personal or collective ideologies."

If culturally responsive teaching supports student learning and helps educators connect to the experiences of students and their communities, why are we still having this conversation? Why aren't we experts in connecting with every child and closing achievement gaps? The reality is that multiple factors impact our abilities to teach and lead in a culturally relevant and responsive way:

> We have **biases** that impact our beliefs and behaviors about students of color and historically marginalized student groups.

> We have **privilege** that impacts the way we view experiences of diverse groups, especially if we are part of a dominant group in education: white and female.

> The **standard curriculum** is taught through a specific **lens**, a lens that often excludes the perspectives and paradigms of culturally and linguistically diverse voices.

> We fail to build strong **relationships** with our students and families, especially if they don't look like us.

These factors are just a few. We can begin to turn the tide and support educators and educational leaders in their journeys toward culturally responsive teaching and leading by addressing the four factors mentioned above: our biases, our privilege, the dominant lens in the recommended curriculum, and our failure to truly connect and understand our students and their families.

As an experienced educator and educational leader, I can't imagine teaching or leading in any other way. Culturally responsive teaching and leading is the only way to educate our children—and this goes for all children. It is the transformational lens through which educators must view their classrooms, schools, and districts. Culturally responsive teaching and leading must be the *non-negotiable norm* in education.

Try This

> Mispronouncing a student's name can cut deep and leave a learner feeling like she doesn't belong or isn't valued. Work with the student (or family) to ensure proper pronunciation. Doing so shows you place value in who they are.

> If your school or class is composed of a diverse group of students, continuously celebrate the diversity and strength of the group. Celebrate different family backgrounds and histories. If the makeup of the group is relatively homogeneous, be diligent in bringing in diverse voices and experiences to develop empathy and inclusivity.

> Connect with people in person or on social media who have a different lens than you do and learn about how you can overcome your personal biases to better understand and connect with the students you serve.

> Reflect on the videos and resources from Teaching Tolerance, TEDx, etc., on thomascmurray.com/authenticedu5 to examine your own privilege, bias, and lens.

> Read and reflect on a book such as *Culturally Responsive Teaching and The Brain* by Zareta Hammond or *White Fragility* by Robin DiAngelo.

MOMENTS OF AWE

"Provide an uncommon experience for your students, and they will reward you with an uncommon effort and attitude."
—DAVE BURGESS

Most of today's classrooms are filled with information: textbooks, trade books, video media, and for many, the world's information at a learner's fingertips, granting access to more information than can possibly be consumed in a lifetime. However, in some classrooms, the information is plentiful, but the inspiration to interact with it is scarce. *Personal* and *authentic* learning won't happen if our classrooms are information rich yet experience poor. It is in and through experiences, particularly those captivated by moments of awe, where deeper levels of learning occur.

PERSONAL AND AUTHENTIC LEARNING WON'T HAPPEN IF OUR CLASSROOMS ARE INFORMATION RICH YET EXPERIENCE POOR.

Awe has been described as "an emotional response to perceptually vast stimuli that defy one's accustomed frame of reference in some domain."[11] What have these moments looked like and felt like for you? What moments of awe have you had recently? What caused the onset of such feelings?

People often describe moments of awe when discussing the natural wonders of the world, breathtaking views, or while visiting historic art for the first time. These experiences can make the previously unseen clear and seemingly cause the world to stand still, if even for a moment.

In his video, *Shots of Awe*, Jason Silva eloquently describes these moments.

I think a lot about the contrast between banality and wonder, between disengagement and radiant ecstasy, between being unaffected by the here and now and being absolutely ravished emotionally by it. And I think one of the problems for human beings is mental habits. Once we create a comfort zone, we rarely step outside of that comfort zone. But the consequence of that is a phenomenon known as "hedonic adaptation." Overstimulation to the same kind of thing, the same stimuli again and again and again, renders said stimuli invisible. Your brain has already mapped it in its own head, and you no longer literally have to be engaged by that. We have eyes, yet see not, ears that hear not, and hearts that neither feel nor understand ... So how do we mess with our perceptual apparatus in order to have the kind of emotional and aesthetic experience from life that we render most meaningful? Because we all know those moments are there. Those are the moments that would make final cut ...[12]

Moments of awe. Moments of wonder. Moments of innate curiosity. Those moments that will make final cut. These moments occur for learners every day in classrooms.

> The kindergartener who reads words for the first time

> The second grader who figures out how magnets work

> The fourth grader who completes the circuit and finally illuminates the light

> The seventh grader who experiences virtual reality for the first time

> The ninth grader who creates something new in the library makerspace

> The high school senior who's in the midst of dissecting a pig in biology class

Stop & REFLECT

What moments of awe occur in your classroom or school? How do the learners respond? Which ones do they remember years later?

As I reflect on my teaching experience, I can guarantee that no child I taught is able to remember a single worksheet I handed out as a classroom teacher. Yet to this day, I'll hear stories about many of the *experiences* that we had together, those moments that some still describe almost two decades later.

That's not to say there's never a time or place for skill building using pencils and paper, as I believe there absolutely is. We just can't pretend that those are the moments that will inspire greatness and unleash the incredible talents found in each one of our learners. We may use those moments as practice but must be realistic about the desired outcomes.

Why is there a difference in long-term memory from my students almost two decades later? Moments filled with awe are personal in nature. They are authentic experiences that tap emotion. Moments of awe create a conduit from what was previously unknown to what can be understood now.

In your classroom or school, what learning experiences inspire moments of awe? Which moments ignite a sense of wonder? Which moments spark your learners' innate curiosity? Which moments will they go home and tell their family about? Which moments will they be able to recall years later?

Which moments will they remember you for?

RELEVANT & CONTEXTUALIZED

"Create relevance, not awareness."

—STEVE JOBS

Each year, I'm blessed to work alongside thousands of educators through our work leading Future Ready Schools® (future-ready.org) and as an author and speaker. From superintendents and other district-level leaders to building principals to those school leaders that teach in classrooms every day, spending time with those who devote their lives to helping children is always a privilege and an honor I never take for granted.

> ### Make It Stick
>
> "Get a puppet. Teach with it. The kids, no matter the age, LOVE puppets. They will ask for the puppet to teach them, and they will be stoked to learn from the puppet. Stoked learning is all we can ask for to start."
>
> —Doug Robertson, elementary school teacher, Oregon

In doing this work, I'm able to have a lot of conversations, lead a lot of discussions, and ask a lot of questions. When facilitating conversations on professional learning, I'll often ask two questions:

1. "What is the *best* professional learning experience that you've ever had and why?"
2. "What is the *worst* professional learning experience that you've ever had and why?"

Stop & REFLECT

How would you respond to those two questions about your professional learning experiences?

Regardless of where I am or the audience I am with, whether superintendents or teachers, the responses are almost always identical. One response in particular is shared when answering both questions—relevance. Among the thousands of educators who have answered those two questions for me, relevance transcends both the best and worst experiences in virtually every conversation.

Can you relate? Were your best professional learning experiences ones that were most relevant for the work you do every day? Did some of your worst experiences include times where there seemed to be a complete lack of relevance to your work, yet you were required to be there?

It should be no surprise that our students can relate to both of those feelings. If students understand the relevance, they probably feel like you do. If students don't understand the relevance, they also probably feel like you do in those moments.

Relevance and a context as to *why* the learning is important propels *personal* and *authentic* experiences. Without a connection to the why, learning is easily stifled.

Relevant learning experiences are those that are applicable to a learner's everyday world. These experiences often tap into a learner's aspirations and solidify a sense of meaning in the world around him or her. When the experience is relevant, learners can articulate a response to the all-too-familiar question, "Why am I learning this?" Relevant experiences often increase intrinsic motivation and inspire one's natural curiosity and wonder.

WITHOUT A CONNECTION TO THE WHY, LEARNING IS EASILY STIFLED.

Contextualized learning experiences are those in which the learner can rationalize how the learning fits in the context of what they already know about the world around them. In essence, learners leverage their own experiences to construct meaning from new information. During these experiences, learners can adequately respond to the question, "What does this learning mean?" Contextualized learning experiences deeply value the context of the individual learner and the lens through which they see the world. Cultural, socioeconomic, and family dynamics are a few examples of how the context in which a learner experiences something will differ.

Let's take math, for example. In my experience, people seem to be overly positive or negative when reflecting on their own abilities or confidence levels in math. The phrases "I'm not a math person" and "math isn't my thing," are relatively common. Would you agree?

It's no secret that one's confidence directly affects students' interest levels when learning content such as math, and there's certainly a connection between one's confidence and motivation. Confidence and motivation undoubtedly have direct ties to one's previous experience as well as an understanding of the relevance of any particular area, whether it be for the growth of students or staff. When learners understand the why and the how, the what becomes that much more feasible. It in no way means the learning will be easy or that the why automatically brings about the learning; however, it increases the connections to what's currently understood, and these types of connections are the basis upon which deeper levels of learning are built.

Subjects like math, loved and despised by many alike, are abstract in nature. Concepts can be difficult to grasp and, depending on how they're explored, can seem completely unrelated to the outside world. It is why teachers must invest time to help learners understand the usefulness of the content. Helping students grasp the real-world application to increase the understanding of the usefulness of information can help fuel the necessary confidence and motivation to learn what's needed.

Relevant and contextualized learning experiences take on many forms and can look drastically different from one place to the next. From the local farmer sharing with the elementary students to the high school senior completing a year-long internship at the nearby hospital, these experiences can take different amounts of time and have different learning outcomes, yet one thing remains common: the *personal* and *authentic* nature in which they take place.

Similar to internships, study-abroad programs, field trips, assemblies, or great hands-on lessons in the classroom, relevant and contextualized learning also occurs during service-based experiences. And service-based experiences—working for and giving to others—can be life-changing.

> ### Make It Stick
>
> "Participation is the only persuasion I use to get my students excited about science. Life is an engaging learning experience, so our classrooms need to be too!"
>
> —Derick Budke, high school teacher, Kansas

Minnesota toddler Cillian Jackson has a rare genetic condition that affects his mobility. At two years old, the boy struggled to move independently. His parents could not afford to purchase an electric wheelchair, which can cost up to $20,000, to assist him, and their insurance would not cover it. With a deep desire to get their son the help he so desperately needed, Cillian's parents reached out to nearby Farmington High School and its first robotics team—known as Rogue Robotics—to see if they could help.

The high school team quickly stepped up to the challenge and opportunity to support one of its own community members. They partnered with GoBabyGo, an organization at the University of Delaware that modifies toy vehicles to give children with disabilities mobility. Accustomed to building their own robots for competitions, the team understood the greater purpose in this particular project.

The work was relevant and contextualized. The experience was undoubtedly *personal* and *authentic*. The team wasn't designing and creating to earn points at an event. They were using their talents to improve the life of a child in their community.

After working for a few weeks and just before Christmas of 2018, the Rogue Robotics team gave Cillian his own customized electric chair and posted an emotional video of him using it for the first time on the team's Facebook page.[13]

 Rogue Robotics - Farmington
December 20, 2018 · 🌐

Our secret is out! For the past few weeks our team dedicated themselves to make a wheel chair for Cillian. We'd like to give a special thank you to Cillian's parents for reaching out to us and giving us such an amazing opportunity! We'd also like to thank our mentors who helped us get it done right before the holidays! What a terrific way to end our preseason!

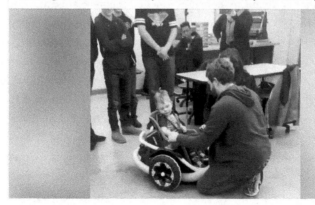

Today's learners are incredible. They are often capable of far more than we empower them to become. When they understand the relevance and are given the opportunity to connect to the context of lessons in their own ways, amazing things can happen.

Stop & REFLECT

What experiences happen in your classroom or school that are relevant and contextualized? How do you know? What would your students say?

IN PRACTICE

MICHAEL McCORMICK, SUPERINTENDENT, VAL VERDE UNIFIED SCHOOL DISTRICT, CALIFORNIA

Val Verde Unified School District (USD) believes in an interdisciplinary and applied approach to learning where rigorous academic concepts are coupled with real-world, problem-based learning. Our school district emphasizes a comprehensive curricular approach to learning that encompasses concepts of science, language, and technology.

The Next Generation Science Standards (NGSS), as defined by the National Research Council (NRC), were created with the goal of blending scientific content with the critical thinking and communication skills needed in a world that is fueled by constant innovations in science and technology. Val Verde USD is dedicated to ensuring our students have a blend of the knowledge and skills that are integral components of a scientist's or engineer's daily work. All Val Verde students have access to learning experiences that involve problem-solving, critical thinking, and collaboration as outlined in the NGSS.

Input from our teachers made us realize that we had to change the support structure and spaces needed to facilitate student creativity. We responded by creating STEAM (science, technology, engineering, art, math) labs in all of our elementary and middle schools. These school sites were given autonomy to design a space that would be highly flexible and focused on using technology to engage students in authentic, solution-oriented learning opportunities that incorporated the engineering design process.

The STEAM labs provide a space where students can experience *personal* and *authentic* lessons that are grounded in content standards and allow students to experience relevant and contextualized learning. In these engaging spaces, students use technology as a tool rather than a goal. Students use robotics, Chromebooks, iPads, 3D printers, CAD design, green screens, LEGO bricks, and cameras to demonstrate their creativity and critical thinking while communicating their unique knowledge contribution to solve real-world problems. Val Verde believes that focusing on STEAM careers early in a child's education will assist in recruiting more girls and minorities into STEAM-related careers as well.

Image Credits: Val Verde Unified School District, California

AMPLIFYING INTERESTS, PASSIONS, & STRENGTHS

"Passion is energy. Feel the power that comes from focusing on what excites you."

—OPRAH WINFREY

My son and daughter, Caden and Paisley, are very different kids. Her first words came early, his came late. What she is allergic to, he can eat. When she wants to relax, he wants to be on the go. He wants to play sports; she wants nothing to do with them. He's outgoing and tries to make people laugh; she's more reserved and serious. She likes chocolate ice cream; he prefers vanilla.

How is it that two children, who trace identical lines on a family tree and live under the same roof, are entirely different in so many ways, including interests, passions, and strengths?

Stop & REFLECT

If you are a parent, can you relate? As a teacher, have you ever taught siblings who are completely different? What have these experiences taught you?

Each year, children come to our schools with unique perspectives on how they see the world. Each filled with their own hopes and dreams. Each gifted with a vast array of talents and abilities. Each containing a myriad of interests and passions weaved with their own set of skills and lens in which they see the world.

Traditionally in classrooms, some students get the opportunity to amplify who they are, while others do not. Each of these students enters a classroom, led by a teacher with a different personality than the one

Make It Stick

"Students and teachers need space to tell their stories of learning mathematics. Storytelling and personal discovery are the variables that amplify the curiosity and magic of this journey."

—Sunil Singh, math educator, Toronto, Ontario

across the hall, different strengths than their team member next door, and different interests than the building principal.

These differences are what make us unique; they help define who we are as people. As educators, we have a key opportunity each day to give students access to new things that we love and that they may not yet realize they love too. Each day we spend with kids is an opportunity to teach a piece of ourselves through our contagious passion for what we share and who we share it with. Let's face it, if we're not passionate about what we teach, there is no chance our students will be.

Where do we provide students with the same opportunity that we have as educators?

EACH DAY WE SPEND WITH KIDS IS AN OPPORTUNITY TO TEACH A PIECE OF OURSELVES THROUGH OUR CONTAGIOUS PASSION FOR WHAT WE SHARE AND WHO WE SHARE IT WITH.

As a high school freshman, Daniela Orozco could recall how many homeless people she had seen on her way to school that year—only one. Four years later, however, the number had multiplied many times over. In her hometown of San Fernando, California, about twenty miles northwest of Los Angeles, homelessness had increased 36 percent from one year to the next. Daniela and her friends wanted to help those who they'd pass on their way to school, but coming from a low-income community themselves, giving them money wasn't an option.

"That was the starting point for their invention: a solar-powered tent that folds up into a rollaway backpack. The girls and ten others from their high school had never done any hands-on engineering work before, but with the help of YouTube, Google, and trial-and-error, they got it done. They hope that one day, their tent will improve the lives of people experiencing homelessness in their community."[14]

Having hardly known one another before the project, twelve high school girls came together around a similar interest. Each also had a passion to help their community, and with support from their school and DIY

Girls, a local non-profit organization, they did just that. Working six days a week and through breaks in the school calendar, this all-female engineering team invented a solar-powered tent for the homeless with hopes of someday mass-producing them so they can be given to people in need.

These girls had no engineering experience, but they had a passion for the purpose. They had no coding experience, but they had a deep interest in supporting people less fortunate than themselves. They had little knowledge of how to design something so complex, but they had incredible strengths in problem-solving, research, iteration, and perseverance.

Learner voice and choice is part of the intuitive nature of learning. It makes the learners an integral part of the process, as opposed to the process being done to them. Such agency connects who they are to the learning. Amplifying the interests, passions, and strengths in our learners recognizes their beautiful uniqueness and shows that who they are really matters.

What do these types of experiences often look like?

1. **Learner Choice in Content:** Providing learners opportunities to select content of interest while still obtaining the desired outcomes is something that frequently occurs in many classrooms.

2. **Learner Choice in Resources and Tools:** Having the opportunity to analyze and select the appropriate resources and tools for the learning goals is often a first step in developing learner agency.

3. **Authentic Assessment Opportunities:** With a goal of demonstrating if the essential knowledge and skills can be applied outside the classroom, these assessments focus on real-world scenarios and often help drive the experience.

4. **Genius Hour:** Students are encouraged to explore their own passions through choice in what they learn during a set period of time during school. Originally modeled after Google's "20% time"

Make It Stick

"Choice is powerful for both teachers and learners. An old school tic-tac-toe board that gives options for classroom activities or professional learning choices empowers everyone and shows that we value them and their unique needs."

—Derek McCoy, middle school principal, Georgia

policy, students use a set period (often per week or month) to explore topics that interest them.

5. **Passion Projects:** Similar to Genius Hour, students design and implement passion projects while tapping into their unique talents and areas that bring them joy.

6. **Career and Technical Education (CTE):** Most often offered as full courses, students can explore real-world fields of study, such as construction, nursing, and computer science, while often earning an industry-recognized certification in the process. Traditionally, CTE has provided some of the most *personal* and *authentic* experiences available to students.

AMPLIFYING THE INTERESTS, PASSIONS, AND STRENGTHS IN OUR LEARNERS RECOGNIZES THEIR BEAUTIFUL UNIQUENESS AND SHOWS THAT WHO THEY ARE REALLY MATTERS.

Stop & REFLECT

Where in your classroom or school are students able to follow their interests, passions, and strengths? Are these experiences the norm or the exception?

Expecting children to walk through our doors and desire a "standard" model of education completely ignores the vast differences in interests, passions, and strengths of our learners. Providing opportunities, both small and large, for these learners to explore areas that are meaningful to them recognizes who they are and reaffirms to them that they matter.

IN PRACTICE

UMA PURANI, TENTH-GRADE STUDENT, PARKLAND SCHOOL DISTRICT, PENNSYLVANIA

Since I have been in elementary school, technology and coding have been an integral part of my life. When my father taught coding to younger students, I would often sit in on the classes and observe; in this way, it became apparent that in a learning environment for technology, the boys are extremely engaged and hands-on throughout the process, while the girls tend to hang back until they think they have the perfect answer. As it turned out, all they needed to completely immerse themselves was a little push from someone who understood them. Consequently, I decided to teach a coding class for five- to six-year-old girls using personalized activities like bracelet-making and dancing to help them better grasp the concepts. Soon after, I came across Girls Who Code, a national non-profit organization that works against the same pattern I had noticed. This seemed to be an opportunity that could be nothing but beneficial for girls of the Parkland School District, and the supportive administration agreed.

In the spring of the 2017-2018 school year, administrators Mrs. Tracy Smith and Ms. Samantha Edwards were vital to starting Girls Who Code in the Parkland School District, and they trusted me to lead the Springhouse Middle School club. They also found a student leader for the Orefield Middle School club. The emphasis that Parkland placed on student voice allowed the entire experience to become more *personal* and *authentic* for everyone involved. In just the first year of the club, we had participation from around sixty-five girls, and the next year, interest grew exponentially! There are even more student leaders at the middle schools now, and Parkland School District has been relentless in making sure that the students are heard and their opinions are taken into consideration. I am incredibly grateful that Parkland believed in my abilities to lead the club because that didn't just benefit me; it became clear to other girls that, even as a middle schooler, you can do anything that you put your mind to!

Make It Stick

"Connect with as many students as you can each day, inquiring more about their interests, exchanging funny stories, visiting their places of employment, cheering them on at their games, integrating their hobbies into lessons, allowing for constant self-reflection, and contacting their parents or guardians to celebrate great things happening. To help authenticate your course's major understandings and skills, strive to unleash student talent and empathy in collaborative campaigns to solve messy community problems, both at home and around the globe."

—Joe Reidy, high school teacher, Pennsylvania

Try This

> Plan a lesson with students! Give students the opportunity to share their thoughts regarding the activities, resources, and how to show their learning.

> Give students choice over their topics so they can select something that interests them. Then empower them to select the relevant tools and resources.

> Allow students to demonstrate their learning in various ways. Authentic assessments that leverage student voices allow them to use their strengths when sharing their understanding of a topic or skill.

FROM CONSUMPTION TO CREATION & DESIGN

"We are born makers. We move what we're learning from our heads to our hearts through our hands."

—BRENÉ BROWN

In his video, "Why Consuming Is Necessary for Creating,"[15] John Spencer eloquently dissects how critical consumption is part of the creation process. Spencer outlines a cycle from critical consumers to personal inspiration, leading to creative work:

> "It's easy to think of creating and consuming as if these two actions were diametrically opposed; however, creativity doesn't happen in a vacuum. When you look at makers, they are often critical consumers of the same type of work they create. Master chefs love to explore new food and have great meals. Songwriters make mixtapes of their favorite songs. The greatest architects travel to distant cities and tour buildings to find inspiration. Filmmakers are constantly watching movies, and athletes watch other athletes in their fields to discover new approaches. Fashion designers look at outfits to gather ideas, and writers are constantly reading books . . . . In other words, makers are frequently consuming, but they are doing it with intentionality.
>
> There's often this ongoing cycle that starts with critical consuming. Here you ask questions and seek out new ideas. You're curating information and geeking out on your craft, and this leads to inspiration. It might be a mash-up of multiple ideas, or you might offer a fresh perspective to a known problem. Often, you'll plan and design, but sometimes you play and experiment, and ultimately that leads to creative work. Now, this could be solving a problem or creating a product . . . but the more you create, the better you understand your craft, which leads to a deeper ability to consume critically, where you then find more inspiration, and the cycle continues."[16]

In highlighting the connection between consumption and creation, Spencer intentionally refers to "critical consuming," which indicates an inherent purpose in the task or activity to gain information. Critical consumption has active, thought-provoking components in the process, whereas passive consumption can add to basic prior knowledge at a lower level.

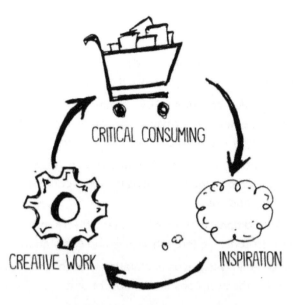

CRITICAL CONSUMING

CREATIVE WORK

INSPIRATION

Image Credit: John Spencer, author and professor

Stop & REFLECT

What does consumption look like in your classroom or school? How is this information most often built upon for deeper levels of learning to occur?

All learning begins with some set of prior knowledge. Recognizing that there are differences in prior knowledge among learners is an essential aspect of *personal* and *authentic* learning, as each child comes to us with a unique background and understanding of any new content we explore. Our five senses allow us to consume information in a variety of ways and lead to different experiences in and among learners. When multiple senses are engaged simultaneously while taking in new information, the experience can become heightened and make what's consumed even more relatable and retainable.

To create *personal* and *authentic* opportunities and deeper learning experiences around new information and ideas, learners must interact with what has been consumed. Following their own inspirations pertaining to the new information, combined with a flexible pace and path to explore and iterate, can put learners in the driver's seat and help them move from critical consumption to authentic creation and design, and that is time well invested.

Try This

> After sharing new content, provide ample time for students to explore the material using a method of their choice.

> Promote "critical consuming" by teaching learners how to analyze and evaluate information they come across. This can be done at any grade level and is an important life skill.

> Help students think through their own device usage and analyze the time spent: consuming low-level content, critically consuming, and creating.

> Alter the traditional method of content delivery and encourage students to consume through inquiry and exploration.

> Focus technology usage on exploration, design, and creativity, as opposed to the over-consumption of content.

FOR LEARNING TO BE *PERSONAL* AND *AUTHENTIC*, WE MUST RESPECT DIFFERENCES IN OUR LEARNERS AND GIVE THEM THE FLEXIBILITY THEY NEED TO THRIVE.

FLEXIBLE PACE & PATH

Life is full of choices. From the moment we get up until the moment we go to sleep, we make conscious decisions, some big and most small. Some estimate that the average adult makes thirty-five thousand decisions per day. As students enter the school building each day, does the number of choices they make go up or down? Why?

With all that we know about how students learn and how the human brain functions, the more obsolete the "lockstep learning model" becomes. Forcing all students to "learn" at a lockstep pace and through a lockstep path, for long periods of time, may be as close to educational malpractice as one can get, but for centuries it has remained the most common learning model.

Fortunately, significant groups of those designing educational structures and experiences today have begun shifting core values, such as the shift in focus from seat time to learning. In these environments, learners are able to advance based on what they know, as opposed to how many hours they spend inside a school building. Some

Make It Stick

"Create a makerspace! Start by creating a personal philosophy for what 'making' means. Plan and design around making principles that engender constructivist learning theories and unleash student creativity with innovative tools and maker project ideas."

—Laura Fleming, high school librarian, New Jersey

places have gone all in, eliminating grade levels and promoting students based upon the mastery of skills, as they work in groups based on ability, aptitude, and interests. These substantial changes take time and require a significant shift in mindset, structure, and high-level policies to be feasible.

On a much smaller scale, there is often conversation around allowing students to "learn at their own pace," and instead of spending most of the instructional time listening to the teacher deliver content to the whole group, students are able to develop skills and explore new information at a pace most suitable for them. It certainly sounds great in theory, yet it can be complex in practice. In districts that institute stringent pacing guidelines (some literally down to the class period), such levels of autonomy and decision-making can be virtually impossible. For learning to be *personal* and *authentic*, we must respect differences in our learners and give them the flexibility they need to thrive.

Every educator can attest to the fact that students learn at different rates, have different skill sets, and need various levels of scaffolding to master concepts and skills. So how can teachers support the natural way the brain learns through flexibility of pace and path with so many restrictions and the "standardization of practice" for kids who are not remotely "standard" by design?

1. **Leverage Adaptive Technologies:** Advances in technology have made unique pacing and paths more feasible each year. With these types of software, learners have the opportunity to accelerate

at the pace at which they are able to demonstrate proficiency in each skill area, and ultimately, beyond their grade level. For those needing additional support, these programs decrease the level of difficulty of the material while scaffolding concepts through explicit instruction, allowing the learner to master the necessary concepts before moving on. It's vital to understand, however, that *personal* and *authentic* learning does not equate to putting a learner behind a device screen all day long. These adaptive technologies are showing tremendous promise and can provide a robust supplemental tool to support the learning but should not be the primary delivery method over sustained periods of time.

Stop & REFLECT

In what ways do you leverage technology to promote a flexible path and pace?

2. **Blended Learning:** When implemented well, blended learning can give learners some control over the pace, path, time, and place, as it's designed for learners to receive part of their instruction through online learning and some through more traditional face-to-face methods. Being technology-rich during instruction does not equate to blended learning unless the learner has some control over where, when, and how they work. In many classrooms, learners have access to a variety of technology tools that ultimately support and enhance traditional instruction, yet in blended environments, the devices are used to make the learning more *personal* and *authentic* through student choice and ownership in the process. Blended learning also has components that occur off-site, such as in a student's home, built into a student's learning path.

Example: Mrs. Addison Thomas is a fourth-grade teacher who uses Google Classroom to post all of her assignments for her students, as they have a one-to-one student-to-device ratio. During the reading lesson, Addison leads her students through a story posted in the online classroom folder. After reading the story together, students use Google Docs to write a descriptive paragraph about what was read and use a digital formative assessment tool to show their understanding.

Was this fictional but realistic example blended learning? No. Was it technology-rich? Yes. In the example above, traditional practices were digitized. From a pedagogical standpoint, there's minimal change from a traditional method that utilizes paper and pencil. Giving learners ownership over where, when, and how would make it more *personal* and *authentic* and yield a more blended experience, ultimately helping them develop agency, a topic we'll dive into further in the final chapter.

3. **Project-Based Learning:** Also commonly referred to as PBL, project-based learning empowers learners to actively explore real-world problems and challenges to obtain knowledge. The goal of these *personal* and *authentic* experiences is to immerse learners in the types of issues and challenges they will face throughout their lives. Using this teaching method enables learners to gain skills by working for extended periods to investigate and respond to authentic scenarios and challenges, which is inherently different from teacher-assigned projects that have been around since the beginning of schooling. Teacher-assigned projects are ultimately about the end product, whereas PBL is about the process and sustained inquiry. PBL experiences are learner-centered, personal, authentic, and provide the learner with a unique path, pace, and ultimately ownership over the experience.

Example: Reilly, a twelfth-grader at the local high school, has chosen to study the effect of pollution on his local community's farmland. Throughout the semester, Reilly collaborates with a professor at the local university, employees of the regional weather channel, and local farmers to understand current levels of pollution and its impact on locally grown crops. At the end of the semester, Reilly presents his findings, which include recommendations of what can be done to support the community's local farms.

Would this fictional scenario be considered PBL? Absolutely. The learner would achieve deep levels of relevant and contextualized knowledge while studying a local, real-world problem. The learner would have significant ownership over the pace and path of the learning and would be learning ways to tackle some of life's challenges throughout the sustained inquiry experience. Although this project would occur over the course of a semester, it's important to note that PBL can occur on a much smaller scale as well.

Example: During a unit on probability and statistics, students are given a variety of topics to explore. Having just passed her driver's test, Lynne chooses to explore issues around texting and driving. She then studies real-world problems and highlights both the issue and the relevant mathematics and presents the findings to a small group of peers. This type of experience allows her to explore relevant interests while simultaneously gaining an understanding of the needed probability and statistics.

Stop & REFLECT

What type of real-world learning experiences occur in your classroom or school?

Leveraging adaptive technology tools and providing blended or PBL experiences are just a few ways that learners can take control of pace and path, providing more *personal* and *authentic* learning experiences. When teachers abdicate some of this control, they must clearly define norms, check in frequently with learners, and set minimum pacing expectations, as self-paced can never mean no-pace. When we empower students to take more control over the pace and path of their learning, we can increase relevance, help develop learner agency, provide more authentic feedback, and create more meaningful, real-world experiences for our learners.

Try This

> Provide a myriad of resources (both digital and print) and encourage learners to choose which resources will best suit their needs throughout a lesson or unit.
> Use diagnostic assessments and reflect on outcomes with students. Have students set individual goals based on the initial assessment results and chart the path to master the needed skills.
> Allow students to skip assessments that measure skills the student has already mastered.
> Leverage adaptive technologies and a mix of digital content for students to supplement their learning. They can decide which resources to use as they move along the learning path.

> For a particular learning outcome, provide a variety of activities and allow each student to choose what is most relevant for them. Embed different formative assessment methods within each choice.

> Flip a lesson by recording the direct instructional component and have students watch that at home. The following day, have students choose from a variety of learning activities and conference with you, diving deeper and ultimately showing their learning. (Note: Ensure students have home broadband access before requiring them to use it.)

AUTHENTIC FEEDBACK

"Words are singularly the most powerful force available to humanity. We can choose to use this force constructively with words of encouragement or destructively using words of despair. Words have energy and power with the ability to help, to heal, to hinder, to hurt, to harm, to humiliate, and to humble."

— YEHUDA BERG

Authentic feedback is at the core of the learning process. Learners need affirmation around their areas of strength as well as guidance and support for their areas of need. Can you remember a time when you received minimal feedback, such as a comment on the top of your paper like "Nice work!" or only a letter grade, such as a B, on the top of your essay? Do you remember a time where you spent a few hours on a homework assignment, only to have a check mark placed at the top of it? Did you find the feedback remotely helpful? Did it authenticate your efforts? Did it amplify

Make It Stick

"Here are five steps to make PBL happen:

1. Show how the standards connect.
2. Don't add to the curriculum; layer it into the curriculum.
3. Assess the process (and only sometimes the final product).
4. What will students make, create, and design? Who are they creating for and why?
5. How can you scaffold and structure the experience?"

—AJ Juliani, director of learning and innovation, Pennsylvania

the great things you did while constructively helping you get better? Of course not, and I'm sure these are examples to which we can all relate.

Stop & REFLECT

When is a time that this type of experience happened to you? What feelings did you have as part of the experience?

Personal and *authentic* learning is a process that reaches maximum effectiveness when useful, relevant, and tangible feedback is left for the learner. Minimal feedback leads to minimal growth. Specific, supportive, authentic feedback with constructive ideas for growth helps students thrive.

John Hattie, a researcher in New Zealand, is well-known for his work and analysis of the "effect sizes" of over two hundred and fifty variables in the classroom, which, of course, include aspects of feedback as it relates to the impact on a learner's growth. In a 2018 *Education Week* interview, Hattie shared, "The key question is, does feedback help someone understand what they don't know, what they do know, and where they go? That's when and why feedback is so powerful, but a lot of feedback doesn't—and doesn't have any effect."[17]

A further breakdown of Hattie's thoughts reveals key reflection questions to help us provide meaningful and authentic feedback to students. Consider the following questions in your work:

> How does the feedback help the learner better understand what they do know?

> How does the feedback help the learner understand what they don't know?

> How does the feedback help the learner understand what to do next?

AUTHENTIC FEEDBACK THAT IS PERSONAL BY DESIGN IS USER-FRIENDLY AND RELEVANT FOR WHERE THAT CHILD IS IN THE LEARNING AT THAT POINT IN TIME.

Hattie's insights help us focus on the aspects of feedback that are most meaningful to the learner. Authentic feedback that is personal by design is user-friendly and relevant for where that child is in the learning at that point in time. It is timely, ongoing, specific, and can occur in a variety of ways. Investing time in authentic feedback can be one of the most supportive things teachers can do, but it must be followed by a meaningful reflection process. Few things are more frustrating for a teacher than spending an incredible amount of time on feedback, only to watch it be tossed in the circular bin a few minutes after handing it back. So how can teachers best provide authentic feedback?

> **Align Feedback to Clear Criteria:** We can all relate to a time we received feedback on something that we weren't aware was being assessed and were left with the feeling of, "If I only knew that's what she wanted!" Authentic feedback can only occur when learners have clear targets they are working toward and an understanding of their purpose in the work.

> **Be Timely and Relevant:** One of the significant drawbacks of today's state-led standardized testing practices is how feedback often takes months to receive, and by the time it arrives,

students are already in the next grade level. When almost a half year has passed, teachers are often left wondering how something from the previous grade level can be beneficial. And who can blame them? The same holds true for our students. Providing minimal feedback, often a few weeks later, has little to no impact on learning outcomes.

> **Focus on Formative:** Formative feedback has a dual purpose. When utilized well, it can provide support for both the learner and the teacher. The learner receives tangible ideas for growth, while the teacher gains a deeper understanding of where to invest his time in the process.

> **Be Actionable:** Feedback that helps learners understand what to do next or is specific in how to improve what is celebrated, naturally creates action steps for progress and clarity in direction.

> **Create a Safe Space for Reflection:** Learners need a space for reflection and trust building for the feedback to be able to support growth. We've all witnessed students who didn't do well quickly place their work in their desks out of shame or fear of the embarrassment of others seeing it. Creating a safe place for students to reflect and to have personal, quiet conversations with the teacher can be difficult yet must be considered.

Stop & REFLECT

What types of feedback do you give your students or staff that is most meaningful? What evidence do you have?

When aligned to criteria the learner understands, feedback that is timely, relevant, specific, and actionable enables reflection and opportunities for learner growth. Learning that is *personal* and *authentic* promotes this process.

Try This

> Be sure to reference a specific skill or knowledge base when giving feedback. The more specific you are, the more actionable students can be.

- Leverage various forms of feedback, such as written and verbal, use of video capture for reflection, as well as artifacts and portfolios, to show growth over time.

- Celebrate growth! How would the culture of your class change if you made one to two positive phone calls home to celebrate one or two students' growth each day?

- Host a one-on-one conference. Although much more challenging at the secondary level due to the number of students, any opportunity to converse one-on-one with a learner can support their growth.

- Deliberately give the same assignment to your students as a colleague in your grade level or in your department. Provide feedback in the style you normally would and reflect with your colleague on similarities and differences in what you provide back to students.

- Develop a classroom protocol around peer feedback. Using a process such as "three things I liked, one change I'd make, and one question I have" (or something similar) can help learners analyze the work of others while simultaneously reflecting on their own.

Make It Stick

"Make sure that your feedback isn't couched in opinion or feelings. Don't start the feedback with 'I like' or 'I love.' Instead, start with the skill area you want to acknowledge. Always make sure the feedback is aligned with the success criteria so students know how they are doing in terms of mastery and how they can improve moving forward. The 'how' is extremely important. We can't just identify what is wrong and leave it up to students to know how to fix it."

—Starr Sackstein, educator, New York

A CLOSER LOOK

For a deeper dive into Chapter 5 as well as free tools, resources, and study guide questions, visit **thomascmurray.com/AuthenticEDU5**.

chapter 6

LEVERAGING TOOLS & SPACES
TO AMPLIFY LEARNING

PEDAGOGY IS THE DRIVER. TECHNOLOGY
IS THE ACCELERATOR.

—MICHAEL FULLAN

---

*I*n the spring of 2002, in my second year of teaching, my class had a one-to-one student-to-device ratio. That's right, in 2002, we were one-to-one.

Palm Pilots. Remember those things?

As funny as it sounds now, those devices were the beginning of digital mobility in the classroom. For the first time, these learners had access to a tool that could take pictures, create digital stories, and "beam" information back and forth, both at school and while at home.

In 2002, these devices were new. They were shiny. They were the gold standard of edtech in the classroom (especially when the color ones came out!).

Stop & REFLECT

What was your earliest memory of using educational technology in the classroom? What did you learn in the process?

A few weeks into the pilot project, I had a planned, formal observation. Like any teacher, I wanted to impress my principal. Knowing that he was joining us that day, my lesson plan was well-thought-out. Student engagement was planned throughout. I was going to be using technology the entire time. I just knew he'd be impressed.

Before sharing about the observation, it's essential to know that my principal was an incredible leader. He created a culture of innovation and pushed us to take risks and try new things. He encouraged us to think outside the box and do things differently for kids as he modeled the way in the process. He also didn't get caught up in the fluff and remained focused on high-quality instruction throughout. He understood what it meant to be *personal* and *authentic* as a leader.

The following week came, and my lesson was planned and ready to go. It was a thirty-minute spelling lesson. (Don't judge.) After reviewing the Palm Pilot expectations and the software we'd be using, we dove in. For the majority of the lesson, students practiced their individualized spelling lists with partners. One partner would read another's spelling word, then the other would write the word using the new Graffiti program on the Palm Pilot and beam it back to his or her partner to check and verify the answer.

For the entire lesson:

> Every student was engaged.
> When questions were asked, virtually every student had their hand up.
> Every student was on task and followed all of my directions.
> My lesson plan was followed perfectly, seemingly to the minute.
> Students used the technology the entire time.

After thirty minutes, as a confident twenty-three-year-old teacher, I wrapped up the lesson and sent my kids out to recess. I remember feeling like I had just crushed it. It had gone exactly as I had planned. I was so glad my principal Bill was there to witness it all.

The following day, all fired up, I walked down to Bill's office for the post-observation meeting. I was excited to hear how great he thought my lesson was the day before.

I remember the conversation like it was yesterday. Ultimately, it fundamentally changed my mindset on using technology and its role in teaching and learning. I sat down, and as he always would, my principal made me feel welcomed. As I stated before, he created a culture where people wanted to be, one in which people could take risks. Bill looked at me and said, "So, Tom, how do you think the lesson went?"

I remember being excited to share. "Well, I think it went really well. My kids were 100 percent engaged. The technology was used the entire time. My lesson plan was followed almost to the minute. Kids were on-task the whole time. Honestly, I think it went really well."

He smiled, looked at me, and said, "So, Tom, what were your learning objectives?"

I began, "We wanted to use the Palm Pilots to be able to—"

He stopped me. "No, Tom, what were your learning objectives?"

Maybe he'd misunderstood. So I started again. "We wanted to use the Palm Pilots to—"

He stopped me again. "Tom, let me push you on this. Every time I ask you about learning, you start talking about technology," he said.

Gulp. He was right.

Bill went on, "Tom, were your kids engaged? Yes. One hundred percent of the time? Pretty much. But they were engaged on very low-level learning tasks. Were great management things in place? Absolutely. But what is it that kids actually learned?"

I remember instant humility coming over me. I was ready to celebrate what was thirty minutes of very low-level learning, if any.

He continued. "I really think you created that lesson because the technology *could do something*, not because it was the *best way to learn something*. Could you have done the exact same thing, with no technology, sitting side-by-side, pencil and paper, in only six or seven minutes?"

Wow. Bill was right. I had become hyper-focused on using the technology. Using the technology was my main goal, not the learning outcomes.

Stop & REFLECT

Can you relate to this? Have there been times you created a lesson because of the technology and lost sight of the learning goals? What did you learn in the process?

Now don't get me wrong, I didn't leave that supervision conversation demoralized. I didn't leave that conversation feeling like a failure. I left challenged to try it again but to lead with learning rather than technology. It was one of those supervision conversations that did what it was supposed to do: It helped me look at things differently and, ultimately, change my practice. It reinforced things I had done well (management) but pushed me where I needed to grow (mindset, vision, and remaining focused on the learning).

TECHNOLOGY IS A TOOL, NOT A LEARNING OUTCOME

Today, millions of Chromebooks, iPads, and PCs are found in classrooms around the globe. Over the past few decades, the technology has evolved tremendously to the point where the devices I used during my first few years as a teacher now look like children's toys. Yet the lesson I learned all those years ago as a young teacher, one that would alter my mindset and help me understand, is just as relevant—and may be more needed today than ever before.

Stop & REFLECT

What's the best supervision conversation you've ever had that helped change your mindset or alter an instructional practice? Why was it so good? How does that conversation help you give authentic feedback to your staff or students?

Today on social media, being paperless is celebrated. Today on social media, a "game-changing tool" is glorified. Today on social media, an amazing new app that has to be used will be shared. It's vital to remember, however, that just because something is glorified on social media does not mean it's the right tool for your classroom or for every learning experience.

We can never lose sight, as I did years ago, about the role of technology in the classroom. It's a tool. It's an amplifier. It is not the learning goal. The app, the tool, the device, will *not* be the game changer. What the learners do with the tools for learning is what's effective and, ultimately, what can help make the learning more *personal* and *authentic*.

Inherently, technology is an amplifier. When combined with high-quality instructional practices, it can accelerate and propel *personal* and *authentic* learning experiences. However, when combined with poor instructional practices, it can also speed up the rate of failure. The teacher and the instructional practices are the real difference maker, not the technology.

"Technology will not replace great teachers, but technology in the hands of great teachers can be transformational."
—GEORGE COUROS

Make It Stick

"Technology can allow us to create safe learning environments for all students to find their voice and build their confidence. While some of our learners are naturally more vocal, others need the time and space to synthesize and process material before contributing to the conversation. By embracing the right tech tools, we can reimagine what class discussion looks like and empower all students with a forum that allows their voice to shine."

—Stacey Roshan, director of innovation and educational technology & high school teacher, Maryland

Stop & REFLECT

We need to stop celebrating low-level learning and put technology in its place. It's a tool. It's a support. It's an amplifier. Construction workers don't glorify their new toolsets. They celebrate the progress on the project and, ultimately, the completion of the desired outcome for those whom they are serving. During the supervision process, checking off and sending feedback that "they were using technology during the lesson" can inadvertently celebrate and reinforce low-level instructional practices.

Leveraging technology tools can undoubtedly amplify and expand *personal* and *authentic* learning experiences. We must, however, remain focused on learner-centered outcomes and not become mesmerized by the latest shiny tool, just as I started to do while sitting in my principal's office all those years ago.

NOT ALL SCREEN TIME IS EQUAL

It seems that every year, the argument over screen time hits the news. From the American Academy of Pediatrics to the local parent group, conversations about how much time is too much can be seen from shows such as *60 Minutes* to the front page of the local newspaper. U.S.-based non-profit Common Sense Media estimates that today's teens spend an average of nine hours per day online, while kids between the ages of eight and twelve spend an average of six hours per day online.

Do those statistics give you pause? As a dad and an educator, they certainly do for me.

Like any statistic, however, it's important to dive deeper and not take any statistics at face value. How are these hours being spent? It's estimated that much, if not most, of that time is spent watching television shows on apps such as Netflix and YouTube, listening to music, texting, playing video games, and using social media apps such as Snapchat and Instagram. Known as "passive use," these types of consumption-based activities typically have minimal educational value. This is why we must focus on the "what" and not just the "how much" aspect of the debate.

Passive, consumption-based use occurs when a user consumes digital content with little thought, minimal levels of creativity, and low levels of interaction required to progress to what's next. In the classroom, passive use isn't inherently bad; however, we have to recognize that time spent in this way ultimately leads to low-level learning. The more time we spend on low-level use, the more time we invest in low-level learning, and the more time we spend, in turn, on promoting low-level outcomes. It is why, in the classroom, your lessons can be 100 percent digital, filled with digital content, all while simultaneously being 100 percent low-level. Every day, this type of experience is glorified on social media.

IF WE'RE NOT CAREFUL, THE SAME TECHNOLOGY THAT KEEPS US CLOSE TO THOSE WHO ARE MILES AWAY CAN ALSO KEEP US MILES AWAY FROM THOSE WHO ARE CLOSE.

It's also important to recognize that the overconsumption of technology can have unintended consequences and undisputed negative impacts. If we're not careful, the same technology that keeps us close to those who are miles away can also keep us miles away from those who are close. The consumption-based gathering of information in and of itself is necessary, but the overconsumption of technology can, in turn, leave us disconnected from those around us.

Stop & REFLECT

What has consumption-based use looked like in your classroom or school? How could you have taken that strategy up a level to promote deeper learning outcomes?

Contrast consumption-based use with tasks that require physical engagement and deeper levels of cognitive thought, and the tasks become active. Active screen time is cognitive in nature, forces higher levels of interactivity, and can lead to deeper learning outcomes. Any educator knows that most children respond to activity-based programming that is fun, interactive, and has real-time, meaningful feedback. It is why activities such as coding, creating digital media, or interacting globally are effective, as this type of use leverages the creative side of a child's brain, promoting deeper learning outcomes.

Consuming YouTube videos is low-level. Creating YouTube videos can be high-level.

Consuming digital music is low-level. Creating digital music can be high-level.

Consuming digital worksheets is low-level. Creating digital simulations or interacting with experts in real-time can be high-level.

It's important to point out that watching YouTube videos, listening to music, and working on multiple-choice questions on a device in and of themselves are not bad activities. Students can learn from them, and we will do these types of activities at times in the classroom. We simply have to recognize the level of learning and tailor our expectations of outcomes for such experiences.

Stop & REFLECT

How is most technology-supported time used in your classroom or school?

In the classroom, you can be amazingly innovative with little to no technology and extremely traditional with all possible tech tools at your fingertips. Just because a teacher has moved instruction from a textbook to a digital document or from a pencil to a device does not mean the learning experience is any better. We cannot expect different learning outcomes just because we digitized past practices. Doing the same thing while expecting different results is a textbook definition of insanity. It's imperative to focus on the depth of the learning experience, as my principal reinforced with me, and not the tool when designing a learner experience.

Technology *does not* equal innovation. Changing the practice and leveraging technology to support more *personal* and *authentic* learning experiences than before is the difference maker. This active use of technology yields learning that is *personal* and *authentic* in nature, whereas consumption-based passive use does not. The technology is only as good as the experience in which it's used.

What Type of Devices are in Your Classroom?

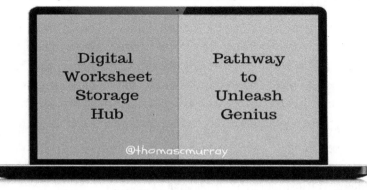

| Digital Worksheet Storage Hub | Pathway to Unleash Genius |

@thomascmurray

IN THE CLASSROOM, YOU CAN BE AMAZINGLY INNOVATIVE WITH LITTLE TO NO TECHNOLOGY AND EXTREMELY TRADITIONAL WITH ALL POSSIBLE TECH TOOLS AT YOUR FINGERTIPS.

Let's dive into one specific example of a tool that has been a hot trend over the last few years: 3D printers. Few will disagree that the idea of 3D printing in schools has gained incredible steam. It's undoubtedly one of the latest bandwagons. Scan social media on any given day, and you'll find end users pridefully holding the most recent "cool" print and hashtagging some synonyms of innovation. Many times, the social sharer touts his or her own innovative ideas, how the tool is a game changer, or how their printer is "revolutionizing learning." Continue to observe, and one can easily understand the notion that because they're 3D printing, innovation is thriving in a classroom, school, or district. Simply put, using a 3D printer does not make one innovative.

While 3D printers can provide students with high-level *personal* and *authentic* learning experiences, they can also be a colossal waste of money and limited resources.

Traveling often and spending most of my time with educators, I've seen four main types of 3D printers in schools. These printers are listed below, as are brief references to their cost, utilization, and ROI—*Return on Instruction*.

1. **"The Bandwagon" Printer**

These printers can often be spotted from a mile away. Walk into the shared common area where it resides, and you'll see the remnants from its ribbon-cutting ceremony. These printers get hyped up from the moment they are delivered and often feel special early on as staff members ooh and ah over the new arrival. After the first few months, however, these printers get lonely and only receive the occasional "hello."

Cost: High
Usage: High at first, then low
Return on Instruction (ROI): Minimal

2. **"The Guinea Pig" Printer**

These printers are typically found in one particular classroom or only one person utilizes it 99 percent of the time (if not 100 percent). These particular printers are used regularly, and materials get reordered often. The issue? These printers serve as toys for the adults, not as tools for student learning. In the vicinity of these printers, you'll notice downloaded directions for the latest cool print, an open browser displaying where the 3D code was copied and pasted from online, a cup of coffee that has been there for a few days, and a myriad of random objects 3D printed in various colors lining nearby shelves. Just like an elementary classroom guinea pig, these pets often get taken home on the weekends by their caregivers so their garage can be converted into a personal weekend makerspace. Pictures of these Guinea Pig Printers and their dollar-store-esque prints get plastered all over social media touting their innovative experiences.

Cost: High
Usage: High (albeit by staff)
ROI: Minimal (sometimes zero)

3. **"The Pop Star" Printer**

Similar to the Bandwagon Printer, these printers often receive a welcome party or at least a faculty meeting happy hour. After the celebration, these printers actually do receive a regular workout. The issue? Student learning is minimal as students spend the majority of the time admiring the pop star on the pedestal. With these 3D printers, full classes of students can venture to the library or makerspace on a field trip. The experience will begin with a teacher sharing how it is a very special day because the students get to "use" the school's new 3D printer. For the next forty-five minutes, students will ooh and ah over the print process. Once complete, the teacher will pull the newly printed lion—or whatever the building's mascot is—out of the printer and hold it high. What do students learn during these pop-star sightings? Almost nothing, except for the fact that 3D printers can print more than text on paper.

Cost: High
Usage: Medium
ROI: Minimal

4. "The MVP" Printer

Finally, a printer that's the real deal and one to write home about. The MVP—the most valuable printer—is used by staff in ways that cultivate *personal* and *authentic* learning experiences for students. These printers understand their role as a team player. They get to share the reward for the hard work that the learner has completed. They understand that they are the finish line at the end of the marathon. These printers get to provide the trophy for the high-level *personal* and *authentic* learning that has occurred during the season and have the scars from the many iterations that have occurred over time. MVP Printers being used in schools are worth every penny. They are viewed as a tool for learning, not as the learning experience itself.

Cost: High
Usage: High (Vast majority of use is by students)
ROI: Medium to high

The vast majority of learning with 3D printers occurs during the design and iteration process, not during the printing process itself. One of my all-time favorite stories around the effective use of edtech that also shares the power of the MVP printer has become known as the "Hand Challenge" (handchallenge.com). To be clear, the story of the Hand Challenge is not about 3D printers. The story is about children changing the lives of other children around the world. It's about learners who were empowered by their teachers to leverage tools to change the world—and they have.

Stop & REFLECT

Can you relate to the examples above? Reflect on a tool that you've seen used for very low-level learning and also used elsewhere for deeper level outcomes. What was the difference between the two experiences?

Chris Craft, PhD, is a long-time educator from South Carolina and one of the founders of the Hand Challenge. His ability to empower students to solve problems is invigorating. His laser focus on learning is a model for what our service to kids is all about. He's also the teacher who inspired his students to dream up the Hand Challenge, something over one thousand schools now participate in.

From the Hand Challenge website:

Officially, the class is called Introduction to S.T.E.M., but unofficially, it's about helping kids find the interests and passions that can propel them through life. We invent, we problem-solve, we learn, and we have a lot of fun. Above all, we're striving to embody the notion that life is not about us. We work towards solving problems in our community and school, such as helping children that do not have two functioning hands.[1]

> ⟲ Hand Challenge Retweeted
> **Chris Craft, Ph.D.** 🔒
> @crafty184
>
> .@americanair This sweet boy had his first plane trip today, raising awareness about limb differences. Check out that 3D-printed prosthetic!
>
> 5:12 PM · Dec 13, 2016 · Tweetbot for Mac

The headline on *People. com* read, "Sixth Graders Make 3D Printed Prosthetic Hands for Kids in Need." The article said, "'They're using their hearts and passion to do something great for this world,' their teacher Chris Craft tells *PEOPLE*."[2]

Like many before him, as a teacher, Chris could have simply enabled his learners to leverage the new 3D printer to create items that could be purchased at the local dollar store. There's certainly nothing wrong with such an activity if students learn throughout the iteration process. Like others, he also could have given all of his learners the

same recipe and directed them to print identical objects by downloading and copying the code and then printing. Instead, Chris inspired his learners to explore, design, and create while simultaneously changing the world and the lives of other children in it.

Personal and *authentic* learning experiences are about people, processes, and pedagogy. When used well, technology tools can amplify those experiences and provide learners with more opportunities and deeper learning outcomes. Examples such as the Hand Challenge mirror what research points to as effective practices, where learners leverage technology to explore, design, and create.[3]

So what does technology use look like in your classroom or school? Is the majority of the tool use active or passive? Are students leveraging technology to explore, design, and create—or to consume?

Today's technology tools are incredible, as many have made instructional practices more efficient and effective. We must ensure that the learning experiences are as well.

Try This

> - Promote student voices by encouraging learners to choose the proper tools for their learning goals. At lower grades, give students the choice of a handful of tools that they have previously used to show their learning.
> - Leverage digital tools for instant formative assessment feedback. Soliciting feedback in real-time gives the teacher data to leverage during the instructional process and pivot when needed.
> - Focus on becoming very comfortable with a few tools that support your desired learning outcomes rather than trying to use many. Your comfort level, combined with your learners' familiarity, can save time on learning the how-tos during class time. It's better to do a few things well than many things poorly.
> - Continuously reflect on the following questions:
>   - » How does this tool accelerate learning?
>   - » Does the technology increase the time it takes to complete the learning outcomes? If so, is the increase in learning worth the additional time?
>   - » Does the technology make the process more efficient and ultimately save instructional time? If so, how will you invest the time that has been saved?

THE EQUITY BARRIER

COAUTHORED BY KEN SHELTON, EDUCATOR, AND EQUITY ADVOCATE

"Treating different things the same can generate as much inequality as treating the same things differently."
— KIMBERLÉ CRENSHAW

Tools and resources to amplify learning are plentiful for many students, but for others, equity in access and opportunity are significant barriers.

The reasons behind such gaps in opportunity are complex. For some learners, it's a lack of opportunities for courses, as schools in underfunded areas can struggle to provide experiences beyond what is required by the state for graduation. For some, it's a lack of the needed resources and tools. For others, it's a lack of access, either due to location or socioeconomic status. For example, many rural schools, which often have far fewer teachers and resources, struggle to provide such learning opportunities on-site. In other cases, the lack of early exposure to such resources or a lack of connectivity at home can be a barrier to a learner's opportunities.

Stop & REFLECT

What equity issues have you seen in your classroom or school? What are you doing to support traditionally marginalized students to close opportunity gaps?

Other areas to further examine when it comes to equity gaps in opportunity are diverse course offerings, the breadth of courses, student enrichment programs, and extracurricular student experiences, such as competitions. For example, one of the most difficult obstacles for schools (especially geographically and socioeconomically challenged schools) to overcome is the volume and actual offering of advanced placement (AP) courses. In this area, gaps can be due to a variety of reasons: arbitrary "minimum requirements," a lack of teacher availability, or a very limited number of teachers with the proper certification (where applicable). Yet these challenges should be tackled head-on, as there are ways in which school leaders can work to overcome them and begin to close opportunity gaps. In high school, for instance, one of the most effective ways, in both cost and geographical accessibility, is to provide students the opportunity to take community college courses or dual credit courses with a university. In many states, students under the age of eighteen can take community college or university dual credit courses for free. This serves as a potential win-win way for schools to effectively close the opportunity gap and benefit students. In many cases, courses can be taken online, which helps address geographical obstacles, and some offer these courses at no cost, which can help address economic barriers. The best part of this type of opportunity is that these courses have a high probability of being directly transferable to any college or university. Access and exposure to these types of classes can effectively broaden the offerings in a school or district without having to explore alternate solutions that may be difficult at best and insurmountable at worst.

Make It Stick

"To promote authentic learning opportunities, have students connect with others, even internationally, and blog about issues that are important to them, such as social justice. Leveraging such tools and experiences can seamlessly foster authenticity. The world can truly be our students' oyster."

—Sarah Thomas, PhD, regional tech coordinator, Maryland

Due to its effective support for high levels of learning and predictions of the future job market, computer science is one example where data points out significant disparities, although progress in recent years has been made. Black, Latinx, and other students from marginalized communities have a lower likelihood of having opportunities in computer science than their Caucasian and Asian peers do. The gaps in opportunity are not only related to race, as females are significantly underrepresented in these areas as well.

In 2016, Black and Latinx people comprised approximately 27 percent of the workforce in the United States, yet only accounted for 16 percent of jobs in STEM-related fields. According to the Pew Research Center, when asked about the underlying reasons why Black and Latinx people are underrepresented in this type of work, 52 percent of those working in

STEM-related fields pointed to a lack of access to quality education that prepares them for those fields, while 45 percent attributed the disparities to not being encouraged at an early age to pursue STEM-related subjects.[4]

Sadly, the trend of who receives support to submit and participate in activities such as robotics competitions, innovation competitions, and design competitions is far too often groups of kids from the same demographic representation. Many schools that are already attempting to overcome geographical and economic obstacles are often not in positions to support student teams for these types of competitions. These gaps can grow considerably if the competition requires long-distance travel. One potential solution school leadership can pursue in this area is to seek out grants and other scholarship-based opportunities from the competition organizers. The organizers could (and should) attempt to tie sponsorship of the competition with a percentage going to schools in need that would benefit from the financial support. In turn, these schools would also be in a position to encourage student participation, particularly those who represent historically marginalized groups. Much of this is dependent on a purposeful intent to close any and all opportunity gaps that exist, both in schools and in the home.

Stop & REFLECT

Evaluate the student demographics that participate in clubs, competitions, and other types of extracurricular activities. Is there a disproportionate representation of student participation in any or all of the groups? If so, what will you do about it?

Furthermore, the "homework gap"—the disparity between those students with internet access at home and those without the needed access—remains a real issue. How large of an issue is this gap? According to the Pew Research Center, most US homes with school-aged children do have the needed broadband. However, when looking at statistics, "most" also implies that some do not. With approximately twenty-nine million households in the United States having children between the ages of six and seventeen, some five million households with school-aged children do not have the needed high-speed internet access at home. Black and Latinx families are disproportionately represented in those statistics.[5]

Stop & REFLECT

Which students in your classroom or school do not have internet access at home? What are you doing to support them?

Whether it's a gap in representation for STEM-related courses, limited access to a diverse set of materials, minimal opportunities for rigorous coursework, or an inability to access needed tools and resources at home, it is our moral and ethical obligation to do everything possible to support each student, particularly those who have been marginalized in the past. How can teachers and administrators best support these learners so that they, too, can have the *personal* and *authentic* experiences provided to their more affluent counterparts? It can be complicated, but it takes three main steps: *know, act,* and *communicate.* We'll look at disparities in access as just one example:

1. **Know the Need:** One must fully understand the need before the problem can be solved. School and district leaders can begin by confidentially surveying families about the access they have at home. As a teacher, if you are assigning work outside of school that includes tasks that require connectivity, you must ensure that learners can actually do what you are asking. In the classroom, it is a moral obligation to remind students who are unable to complete something digital at home to come see you and provide them with equal opportunities. On a larger scale, schools and districts should leverage any needed method to gain an understanding and work to develop a systematic plan of action to support those in need. (Note: Don't just ask *if* they have internet access; ask *how* they connect to the internet if they do. Having to use a cell phone instead of a laptop to complete work can be a very different experience.)

2. **Act on the Need:** Once school and district leaders know the extent of the lack in access, there is an obligation to develop a game plan to provide the needed tools and resources, or a comparable experience at a minimum. Today, schools are leveraging resources such as *EveryoneOn.org*, partnering with businesses, places of worship, or the local municipality, and providing access points in marginalized locations.

Make It Stick

"Close the Hope Gap! There are so many students of lower socioeconomic backgrounds who place limitations on themselves because they see limited possibilities around them. Use video conferencing as a way to expose students to people, places, and ideas outside of their neighborhood so that students can see a broader example of what is possible. This is particularly powerful when students of color can see, engage, and connect with professionals who look like them. When they see excellence in someone who looks like them, they begin to see excellence within themselves."

—Will Deyamport, EdD, instructional technologist, Mississippi

3. **Communicate the Opportunities:** It is vital to leverage a variety of tools to ensure that families understand their options and opportunities—whether through letters home, forms at registration at the beginning of each school year, calls to those who have not responded, or providing the needed information at one's doorstep—meeting families where they are and being sensitive to language and cultural differences. If families don't know of the support available, they won't access it.

Learning can only be *personal* and *authentic* when opportunities exist. Today's tools provide incredible resources for teaching and learning both inside and outside of school, but we must be conscious of gaps in opportunity and work diligently to support those who have been traditionally underserved. Without doing so, we exacerbate inequities. Ensuring equity isn't about checking a box. It's about analyzing the need, developing a plan of action, and getting the work done to provide each learner with access and opportunities. When we avoid addressing equity-related issues, we add to the unwanted patterns of the past.

LEARNING CAN ONLY BE *PERSONAL* AND *AUTHENTIC* WHEN OPPORTUNITIES EXIST.

Great teachers use all the tools and resources available to amplify teaching and learning in their classrooms. They always have. Today's tools can provide opportunities to make the experience more *personal* and *authentic* for the learner, but the space in which the learning takes place is also an important, evidence-based aspect of the learning experience.

Try This

> Analyze which students are taking which courses at your school. Are there disparities in the subgroups of students? If so, what are you going to do about it?

> Explore *EveryoneOn.org*, a non-profit organization focused on getting families connected, to see what's available in your zip code.

> Work with district-level administrators to develop a comprehensive plan to attack the "homework gap" for all of your schools, if one is not yet in place.

> Create a map of your community highlighting all the available free Wi-Fi hotspot locations, such as the public library, Starbucks, McDonald's, etc. Partner with local businesses to offer more.

> Connect with every family in your classroom (elementary) or every student (secondary) and clearly articulate what supports are available if they don't have the needed access at home.

> Principals:

>> Analyze subgroup data to study disparities in discipline rates, attendance rates, and achievement data. Don't simply "gaze at the gap"—work with your team to implement a plan to close it.

» Provide the needed professional learning to help all staff overcome their bias to support students in the way in which they deserve.

» Seek outside support, such as grants, partnerships, and community collaboration, to support those students who have been traditionally underserved.

INTENTIONAL LEARNING SPACE DESIGN

"Learning spaces are the nonverbal story of your school."
—DR. ROBERT DILLON

In recent years, learning space redesign has become one of the trendiest topics in education. Yet not all things glorified on social media are highlighted for the right reasons. Designing learning spaces is about how design impacts the brain and learning, not about being pretty for Pinterest. If the focus on your classroom space is about being pretty and cute, you're caught up in the fluff, those things that don't impact learning.

DESIGNING LEARNING SPACES IS ABOUT HOW DESIGN IMPACTS THE BRAIN AND LEARNING, NOT ABOUT BEING PRETTY FOR PINTEREST.

Stop & REFLECT

Reflect on your classroom space or one in your building. Why was the space designed as it was? What does the space indicate regarding your beliefs about how teaching and learning occur?

Every child needs and deserves to know that they belong, both as a part of the class and in the learning space itself. It's essential for *personal* and *authentic* learning to take place, and as educators, it's our moral and ethical obligation to make that happen. We can only be intentional with our space design if we understand *the why* behind it.

During my first few years teaching, I set up the space for me. There was little to no design to what I created for my learners. The front portion of the classroom space was open, where I would share content, and the space included my rather large, heavy teacher's desk. Similar to many traditional classroom spaces, I set up about one-fourth of the space for me, while my learners had to share the remaining three-fourths of the room. In thinking about those things that I "decorated" the walls with, many of them pertained to my interests and the things that I liked. Those first few years, students had no input into the space itself, although their work was hung throughout, albeit at times for months on end.

Understanding the why behind space design takes an understanding of how design impacts learning. As previously shared in "10 Key Principles" in Chapter 4, "The entire environment, from space to temperature to lighting, can affect learning." Although little research on learning space design was available during my first few years teaching, a lot has been learned since that time.

Clever Classrooms, a report highlighting three years of research on 153 classrooms from twenty-seven diverse schools, analyzed the impact of the learning space on reading, writing, and math achievement.[6] The report concluded a 16 percent variation in learning progress over a year for the 3,766 students in the study, meaning the impact of moving an "average" child from the least effective to the most effective space is significant. The study took into account a wide range of sensory factors and utilized multilevel statistical modeling to isolate the effects of classroom design from other important factors such as the students themselves and their teachers. The key findings of the study were the impact of naturalness, individualization, and stimulation.

1. **Naturalness** considered the effects of lighting, temperature, and air quality, which accounted for about half of the learning impact.
2. **Individualization** considered the ownership and flexibility of the space, which accounted for about a quarter of the learning impact.
3. **Stimulation (appropriate level of)** considered the complexity and color of the space, which accounted for about a quarter of the learning impact.

If we are going to intentionally design spaces to support *personal* and *authentic* learning, we must be conscious of the impact of the space on the learning itself. So what are some evidence-based ways that teachers can maximize the design impact and create more *personal* and *authentic* spaces?

NATURALNESS

> Maximize the amount of daylight that can enter the classroom space. Open the classroom blinds, avoid covering the outside windows with displays, and don't place large pieces of furniture in front of the windows. Remain conscious of any glare that may occur, as glare can have a negative impact.

> Consider all opportunities to improve air quality and temperature in the space. Open windows when feasible.

> Sound-absorbing treatments to a room can be beneficial. Small carpets or rugs, combined with rubber feet on moveable furniture, minimize unwanted sounds.

> Add natural elements in the classroom, such as plants, so students can experience elements of nature throughout the day.

INDIVIDUALIZATION

> For younger students, well-defined "learning zones" can be beneficial for simultaneous activities (e.g., carpet area, reading nook, makerspace area), whereas for older students, a few

zones can support more formal individual or group work while avoiding unwanted clutter.

> Amplifying the students as individuals and highlighting recent student work (including artwork) helps provide a sense of ownership of the space.

> Set aside a space for each child to display and share work. Have students pick what they would like to share and put the student in charge of sharing individual learning and successes in that space.

> Allow students, where appropriate, to personalize aspects of the space. Possible areas include lockers, drawers, desks, coat closets, or high school parking spaces.

> Be conscious of and sensitive to differences in gender, race, and culture in all aspects of the space design.

> Maximize low-cost ways to create and utilize flexible furniture to increase mobility and opportunities for various learning experiences.

> Create a continuous feedback loop for student agency and voice regarding the space.

STIMULATION

> Classroom displays on the walls and anything hanging from the ceiling should provide a lively sense to the space, but avoid being chaotic or distracting. It's recommended that 20 to 50 percent of wall space should be kept clear.

> The use of bold colors or objects should be used as accents to the space and should not consume the space itself.

> Remember that students will respond to stimuli in various ways, so aiming for a "mid-level" of stimulation should be the goal. A sterile, hospital-like feel lacks any stimulation, whereas a space where most of the square footage is consumed would be overstimulating for many.

$Stop$ & REFLECT

How do the above evidence-based thoughts correlate with your classroom or school? What's one change you could make?

Does the space in your classroom amplify a place to explore, design, and create or to consume and regurgitate? Was it designed *for* the students or *with* the students? Does the space empower agency or demand compliance? Does it promote active or passive learning?

Spaces for Passive Learning	Spaces for Active Learning
One large space	Various zones
Immobile	Mobile and fluid
Set structure	Flexible and movable
Limited personal space	Various spaces with personalized aspects
Disconnected	Seamless connectivity and charging for mobile access on demand
Heavy desks	Tables, stations, movable furniture

Personal and *authentic* spaces empower students to create, iterate, and seamlessly collaborate with others. These spaces allow for students to be active participants and not just passive consumers.

When focusing on learning space design, it's easy to get caught up in the latest Starbucks analogy or feel as if the space needs to be "Pinterest-worthy," as so many have glorified these types of spaces on social media platforms. Instead, remain focused on the following:

1. **Prioritize Mindset Before Money:** Before spending limited resources on a given space, focus on the why to ensure the change will have an impact on learning. Throwing money at new furniture in a teacher-centric environment where pedagogy doesn't shift is a complete waste of resources.

2. **Maintain a Common-Sense Mindset:** The day we see bouncy balls in chemistry class or a beanbag chair for the tuba player, we'll have completely lost our minds. Don't lose common sense or get caught up in the latest trend during the design process.

3. **Include Spaces to Explore, Design, and Create:** Even if classroom square footage is limited, a "creative corner" or a small makerspace table can stimulate curiosity and inquiry-based learning.

4. **Maximize Flexibility, But Do So with a Purpose:** Flexible seating can either be an excellent support for student agency or a trendy disaster in the making. Flexible seating is about student choice and agency, not about forcing all kids to sit on bouncy balls or beanbag chairs. In a more learner-centric environment, flexible seating can promote voice and choice while increasing comfort, something we all desire.

5. **Think Multiuse for All Purchases:** In most classrooms, space is difficult to come by. Flexible furniture can support various zones and can be moved quickly to adjust spaces on the fly. Maximize the dollars you do have by purchasing items that can serve a variety of purposes. For example, a lightweight table on wheels may also serve as a storage container for classroom supplies.

Learning spaces are only as effective as the impact on those who utilize the space. To ensure that we maximize the impact for each student, we must maximize the inclusivity of the space as well.

INCLUSIVE SPACES

"Inclusion is more than a set of strategies or practices; it is an educational orientation that embraces differences and values the uniqueness that each learner brings to the classroom."
—PAULA KLUTH

Personal and *authentic* spaces are inclusive by design. To create inclusive spaces, we must consider and amplify the importance of individualization, both the research outcome and the understanding that each of our brains is uniquely organized. As such, we perceive the world in different ways. Because of this, people respond to environmental stimuli in various ways. Therefore, the opportunity for some level of choice impacts success.[6]

Stop & REFLECT

How do inclusive spaces correlate with Maslow's Hierarchy? Is the space that you design inclusive for all learners? How do you know?

In a late 2018 #LeadershipMinute, a one-minute video that I share each week, I asked Dr. Adam Phyall, director of technology and media services for the Newton County School System in Georgia, about how we can best create inclusive spaces. In the video, Adam shares the idea of creating "watering holes, campfires, and caves," which are terms used to describe how to set up zones of space for different activities.[7] For instance, a "watering hole" is an informal space set up for learners to share information and a place where all learners can have an equal say. In these spaces, some may assume the role of the teacher and others the role of the learner at various times throughout the experience. A "campfire" is a space where people gather to learn from an "expert" in the class. Storytelling is one example of communication that may occur here. Finally, a "cave" is a reflective, often quiet, space where a learner can think and work independently. Each of the spaces is intended to be flexible in nature. Students can move to different places based on the task at hand. Adding watering holes, campfires, and cave spaces to your classroom can enable a more *personal* and *authentic* experience for the learner.

The understanding of "individualization" from research and the learner being valued as an individual, is central to inclusive and intentional space design. It's also impossible to be inclusive without being conscious of gender, race, and culture. Consider these two common scenarios:

> ### *Make It Stick*
>
> "Ask your students what they hope for the space and let them work through the design process. It's just as much their classroom as it is yours."
>
> —Kayla Dornfeld, elementary teacher, North Dakota

Scenario 1: Kayden, a six-year-old boy in kindergarten, walks into his classroom each morning, a space consumed with pink, purple, polka dots, flowers, and chevron print. Each day as he enters, he thinks how much he despises those "girl" colors that his sister likes.

Scenario 2: Jada, an African-American female in eleventh grade, walks into her U.S. history classroom space each day and sees walls covered in images of "success" from her country's history, but all the people depicted are white men.

Do the learners feel a sense of belonging in these fictional scenarios? Do they see themselves as vital parts of the space? Are these spaces inclusive? Are they *personal* and *authentic* by design? Certainly not, yet these are common, everyday examples.

It's imperative that educators consider such scenarios and actively ensure an inclusive environment so all students feel welcome in their learning spaces. It's impossible to be *personal* and *authentic* when people don't feel like they belong. Intentionally creating inclusive spaces is not a "nice to have" option; in fact, it's grounded in the learning sciences. It is our moral obligation to ensure that every child feels welcome and has a sense of belonging to the group and the space.

When working to create inclusive spaces, consider the following:

Tip #1—Ask colleagues of the opposite gender to provide feedback. Remaining gender-neutral in space design should be a goal.

Rule of Thumb: If a learning space is viewed as overly male or female, it needs to be reassessed and made more inclusive of the opposite gender.

Tip #2—Ask colleagues with different cultural backgrounds (e.g., race, ethnicity) or have different beliefs from you (e.g., religion, politics) to give you honest feedback about your space and how to make it more inclusive. Ask them what you can do to make others feel a greater sense of belonging.

Tip #3—Ensure that classroom resources and libraries are intentionally diverse. Recent years have seen a significant emphasis on ensuring learners have access to diverse literature. Can students "see" themselves in the available literature? Are the characters reinforcing stereotypes or breaking stereotypes and boundaries?

Tip #4—Ask the learners what they think! Too often we work to solve problems without asking those whom the decisions impact. When

> ## Make It Stick
>
> "Consider removing large bays of lockers to create open, flexible spaces that can be used as common areas and extensions to classrooms. Leverage student voice as part of the process."
>
> —Dwight Carter, NASSP digital principal, Ohio

designing an inclusive space, focus on the why and leverage the feedback of those who will use the space regularly. Remember, it's not "my" space; it's "our" space.

In both cases, honest feedback may strike up some difficult, but necessary, conversations. Having empathy for others with different life experiences and reflecting on our own mindsets are essential aspects of growth as an educator. Sometimes it's our own lens that gets in the way. Sometimes our lens prevents us from redefining what's possible.

SOMETIMES IT'S OUR OWN LENS THAT GETS IN THE WAY. SOMETIMES OUR LENS PREVENTS US FROM REDEFINING WHAT'S POSSIBLE.

Stop & REFLECT

What do your learners think about your space? Have you asked? Have you leveraged the learners' voices to improve the inclusivity of your space?

IN PRACTICE

ADAM PHYALL, EdD, DIRECTOR OF TECHNOLOGY AND MEDIA SERVICES, NEWTON COUNTY SCHOOL SYSTEM, GEORGIA

First, let me say that I am not an expert on inclusive learning spaces. I just know that the work I am doing is having a positive impact on the students I serve. I am working to include as many students as possible in our library learning commons. The media centers in the school district have changed very little over the past twenty years, but the population and needs of the students have changed drastically.

My school district experienced a tremendous decline in student usage at the secondary level. Like most school systems, this begins the time when students are not required to go to the media center to check out resources. This is actually a time when students need to be engaged in authentic literacy opportunities. When I began my role as supervisor of my system's library media program, it was obvious a change was needed to have a positive impact on all of our students. The change that we wanted to create was more than just some rolling tables, a new coat of paint, or some DIY projects. We wanted to create more than just a fancy space; we wanted an *inclusive space.* We wanted a space where our stakeholders would want to spend the whole day enjoying the resources. We wanted to have resources that reflected our students' diverse needs and interests. We wanted to provide our stakeholders with a chance to have a voice in their media center.

We set out to gather as much stakeholder data as possible to understand their thoughts and beliefs about the library learning commons. We wanted to hear from not just the students that were currently utilizing our media center but also the students that were avoiding it like the plague. After speaking with students, parents, and staff, it became apparent to us that we had to develop a clear and concise district media center collection plan. The plan reflected the school district's efforts to promote literacy and reading at all levels. Using data collected, stakeholder interest and library checkout trends allowed the media centers to purchase resources that met the needs of our diverse learners. The information provided a wave of transformation that impacted learning throughout the school district. We found it refreshing to see students in our library media center that had not visited in years. During our process of creating a more inclusive space, I tried to be as honest as possible with my team. I realized that we have not reached our goal of having 100 percent of our students utilize our library learning commons, but when I now look at the number of students who are actively seeking out our library learning commons, it tells me we are on the right track.

Make It Stick

"The research continues to emerge that intentional classroom design has a powerful impact on the emotional well-being and the academic success of all students. This begins with providing more opportunities to move, increasing student choice about where they learn, and continuing to get feedback from students on how the space is serving them."

—Robert Dillon, EdD, director of innovative learning, Missouri

Try This

> Begin the school year by having parts of your classroom remain a blank canvas so students can help create the space. Use "Under Construction" tape to emphasize the point!

> Visit other spaces and informally interview the teachers who helped design them. What aspects of the spaces are different and why were they designed that way?

> Work to create a space that promotes movement, allows for various groupings, and enables hands-on exploring, making, and designing.

> Leverage social media for ideas and possibilities. Tools such as Twitter, Pinterest, Instagram, and Facebook can be great avenues to explore possibilities and find great "hacks," but beware of ideas that stray from the purpose of the work.

> Objectively analyze the images that create the classroom perimeter for both race and gender. Reflect on the current makeup of images and act on it to ensure an inclusive space.

> Ask a colleague with life experiences different than yours for honest and constructive feedback. Don't be offended by their responses; act on them.

A CLOSER LOOK

For a deeper dive into Chapter 6 as well as free tools, resources, and study guide questions, visit **thomascmurray.com/AuthenticEDU6**.

chapter 7

CREATING A LEGACY THAT IMPACTS A LIFETIME

THE BEST THING ABOUT BEING A TEACHER IS THAT
IT MATTERS. THE HARDEST THING ABOUT BEING
A TEACHER IS THAT IT MATTERS EVERY DAY.

—TODD WHITAKER

———

eing an educator is incredibly hard work. It takes an unbelievable amount of courage and strength to do the work well. You give and you give and you give, sometimes until you have nothing left. You work tirelessly for others, devoting your life's work to helping others, and as discussed in Chapter 2, you must simultaneously work diligently to invest in yourself—through your own self-care. We cannot invest ourselves so much into the lives of others that we have nothing left for our own families or lose ourselves in the process. The work is too important—you are too important—for that to happen.

Who's that child for you? Who's the child that caused you vast amounts of frustration early in the school year? Who's the child that causes you to question your effectiveness as a teacher? Who's the child that causes you to lose sleep at night? Did you ever think that maybe, just maybe, he or she are in your classroom or school for a reason? Maybe you are the teacher that helps him or her find their purpose in life. Maybe you are the teacher that helps give him or her the direction they need. Maybe you are the only safe place that child has each day they are with you. Maybe you are the teacher that they'll tell their own children about—the teacher that helped them turn it all around.

As you continue on your journey to make your relationships, culture, and learning experiences *personal* and *authentic*, don't expect perfection—from yourself or from others. It'll only lead to disappointment. Know that things will happen that cause you to struggle. It's not if, but when. Those times will take perseverance and resilience to carry you through. The times you fail will be opportunities to pick yourself up and try again, with a better understanding than before. Along the way, you must celebrate the many successes and take pride in the work you do as an educator. Your work, every day, matters. You are designing learning experiences that impact a lifetime.

YOU ARE DESIGNING LEARNING EXPERIENCES THAT IMPACT A LIFETIME.

PERSEVERANCE & RESILIENCE

"You're always going to have critics and naysayers and people that are going to tell you that you won't, that you can't, that you shouldn't. Most of those people are the people that didn't, that wouldn't, that couldn't."
—TIM TEBOW

The NFL Combine is an event where college football players who want to play professionally perform both physical and mental tests in front of coaches, scouts, and general managers. Tests include the 40-yard dash, a vertical leap, and a 225-pound bench press, among others. In educational terms, it's the "summative assessment" of a player's physical attributes and skill at the culmination of his college career and provides indicators as to whether or not a team should select a player in the upcoming NFL draft.

At the 2000 NFL Combine, a young quarterback from the University of Michigan measured poorly on many of the standardized testing metrics. He ran the 40-yard dash in 5.28 seconds, much slower than his competition. His 24.5-inch vertical leap was much less than the almost 32-inch average of an NFL quarterback. He chose not even to complete the 225-pound bench press test. Scouting reports after the combine were filled with every reason this quarterback should not be drafted by an NFL team. One scouting report highlighted the drawbacks to this player:

Negatives: Poor build. Very skinny and narrow. Ended the '99 season weighing 195 pounds and still looks like a rail at 211. Looks a little frail and lacks great physical stature and strength. Can get pushed down more easily than you'd like. Lacks mobility and ability to avoid the rush. Lacks a really strong arm. Can't drive the ball down the field and does not throw a really tight spiral. System-type player who can get exposed if he must ad-lib and do things on his own.[1]

This quarterback was passed over by every team five times during the 2000 NFL Draft. One hundred and ninety-eight other players were drafted before him. It took until the sixth round, one of the last rounds of the draft, for him to be selected.

Nineteen years later, this quarterback has won four Super Bowl MVP Awards, the most ever by a player. He is a three-time league MVP and has been selected to fourteen Pro Bowls, the NFL all-star game. He has more postseason passing yards and touchdown passes than any other quarterback to have played the game. His name is Tom Brady.

What didn't the standardized testing at the NFL Combine measure? The tests used for all players leading up to the draft couldn't measure Tom Brady's work ethic. They didn't measure his fierce competitiveness or his leadership abilities. No test at the NFL Combine measured Brady's ability to persevere, his resiliency, or his burning desire to win. It is these things—things that weren't measured and couldn't be measured by a standardized test—that have made Brady one of the greatest NFL players of all time.

How many of our students can be viewed in a similar light? How many students may score poorly on a particular assessment yet have the necessary qualities to succeed in life? Are teachers ranked by their teaching certification test scores once they finish their degrees? Do the highest scores on a state teacher certification exam always make the best teachers? Of course not.

Stop & REFLECT

Are you thinking of particular students right now? How did those children's perseverance and resilience lead to their success? How did you support them in the process?

Whether leading in the classroom or leading a school, obstacles and adversity will come our way. The longer we're in the profession, the more adversity we'll experience. If you're new to the profession, just ask a veteran colleague. As much as we may like to, we don't get to choose what happens outside of our circle of control as we push forward in the work. It often seems that the more we step outside of the status quo, the more adversity stares us in the face. We may not get to choose the difficulties we face, but we must face those difficulties to move forward in the work. What we do get to choose, however, is our internal reactions, our external responses, and what we'll learn from the experience.

WE MAY NOT GET TO CHOOSE THE DIFFICULTIES WE FACE, BUT WE MUST FACE THOSE DIFFICULTIES TO MOVE FORWARD IN THE WORK.

Few people exhibit the perseverance and resilience that's shown by educators teaching in classrooms and leading schools every day. As a teacher, leaving a lasting legacy takes this type of perseverance and resilience. Being an effective administrator and modeling the way while supporting your staff and students also takes this type of perseverance and resilience. For our students, it is through *personal* and *authentic* learning experiences where the life skills of perseverance and resilience can best be learned, and it's up to us to make it happen.

Stop & REFLECT

How do you model perseverance and resilience to those around you? What *personal* and *authentic* learning experiences do you oversee that promote the growth of these life skills?

FAILING FORWARD

"There is no innovation and creativity without failure. Period."
—BRENÉ BROWN

As a teacher, and later as a school and district-level leader, I failed often. I often reflect on one time in particular.

I was looking back through my notes as I sat next to one of my teachers in a post-observation meeting. As her principal, I was about to give feedback on her lesson from the previous day.

Two days prior, I had run our team's faculty meeting after school. As a newer principal, so many of these meetings had looked the same. They were one-directional and primarily used to disseminate relevant information (that could have been an email), complemented with the occasional team discussion. Let's face it, there is a tremendous amount of managerial things that must get accomplished for a school to run smoothly. This particular faculty meeting wasn't much different than those I had run in the past.

That Monday afternoon, for sixty straight minutes, I mostly talked at my team. Although there were some topics for discussion, in retrospect, the faculty meeting was a one-directional monologue on everything they needed to know and do the coming month.

We need to do this, and we need to do that.

You'll have to do this, and you'll have to do that.

. . . and so on.

The following day, I had a scheduled observation. I showed up as planned, took notes throughout the lesson, and worked through what I typically would, looking to highlight areas of strength and ways to give *personal* and *authentic* feedback on what could make things even more effective.

For this particular lesson, the teacher lectured for the vast majority of the period. Although some humor was used, some student reflection occurred, and a few good stories were told, the lesson was primarily one-directional. So in my notes, I wrote:

"When we have a captive audience for sixty straight minutes, we need to get them engaged, have conversations, and get them moving. For the most part, this particular lesson was primarily one-directional."

So there I was, sitting next to her as we talked about the previous day's lesson. Once I had highlighted some positives that had occurred, I looked through the notes I had written the day before and began to feel nauseous.

I started to realize that I was about to tell her not to do *precisely what I had done* to her and our team on Monday. Feeling sick to my stomach and like a complete hypocrite, I said, "So one of the pieces of feedback I was going to give you to work on is that when we have a captive audience, especially for sixty straight minutes, it really needs to be more than one-directional . . . but I can't end that sentence without saying it's also exactly how I ran our faculty meeting on Monday. How can we both get better at that?" I'll admit, as a principal, calling out your own poor practice to a teacher is humbling. However, I began to realize that when it was on me to plan things, I hadn't always modeled what I was asking my teachers to do. When it was my turn to lead something (such as a faculty meeting), I would sometimes do it in a way that was the complete opposite of what I was asking of my teachers. In those instances, I wasn't living my expectations of others.

Stop & REFLECT

Have you ever felt like you weren't modeling what you asked your students or staff to do? How did you remedy the situation?

To build relationships with others, we must model the desired behaviors. To build trust, we must model the desired interactions. As educators, every time we bring people together, it's an opportunity to model what we're asking for from others.

Every faculty meeting is an opportunity to model learning that's personal. Every in-service day is an opportunity to model fun, authentic learning. Every time students are passing in the hallway, it's an opportunity to model what it means to be present. Every time a principal speaks to a teacher, it's an opportunity to model what good listening looks like and what empathy feels like. Every time a teacher speaks to a child, it's an opportunity to model how to treat others with dignity, respect, and love.

EVERY TIME WE BRING PEOPLE TOGETHER, IT'S AN OPPORTUNITY TO MODEL WHAT WE'RE ASKING FOR FROM OTHERS.

As teachers, if we are going to ask something of our students, or as principals, if we are going to ask something of our team, we must also be modeling it ourselves. Anything else is hypocritical. It's saying one thing and doing another, something we've all been guilty of at one time or another. It was the exact feeling I had that Wednesday morning during the post-observation conference.

I think most educators are wired to be perfectionists, and that fear of failure is a natural byproduct. Because of how their brains seem to be wired, most educators expect things to be perfect the first time. Whether it's the lesson plan, the professional learning session, or the conference presentation, they want it to be just right. It's how so many educators are, and that's because most have high expectations—of themselves and of others. (That's something we should never change.)

We also have to understand that, as humans, we're going to mess things up. We're going to make a bad call. A lesson will fail. A presentation will flop. We'll say the wrong things to a student or a parent. It happens, and it's going to happen again—not just to us, but to those we work with and those we serve. Failure is an opportunity for a fresh start, only with more profound knowledge and understanding than you had the last time.

Walt Disney, one of the greatest entertainers to ever walk this earth, was fired for not having original ideas and for "lacking imagination." The Beatles, rejected by Decca Recording Studios, were told they had "no future in show business." Lucille Ball was called "the Queen of B Movies" due to her long string of low-rate films at the start of her career. Albert Einstein was unable to speak until he was four. In school, his teachers said he'd "never amount to much."

FAILURE IS AN OPPORTUNITY FOR A FRESH START, ONLY WITH MORE PROFOUND KNOWLEDGE AND UNDERSTANDING THAN YOU HAD THE LAST TIME.

These incredible individuals could have given up. They could have let self-doubt become the driver of their decision-making. But they didn't. They learned from it. They owned it. They failed forward, and today they are household names.

What's another key difference in those who fail forward?

Mindset.

Michael Jordan, by far one of the greatest basketball players to ever step on the court, was cut from his high school basketball team. As we all know, his career in the sport would go on to forever be recognized as one of the best. In a 1997 Nike commercial that highlighted Jordan's career, he shared:

"I've missed more than 9,000 shots in my career. I've lost almost 300 games. 26 times, I've been trusted to take the game-winning shot and missed. I've failed over and over and over again in my life. And that is why I succeed."[2]

"I've failed over and over and over again in my life. And that is why I succeed." These are amazingly powerful words. How can we build such a culture of failing forward in our classroom or in our school? As teachers and administrators, how can we model this type of mindset to those we serve?

Stop & REFLECT

When's the last time you failed forward? How were you impacted by the experience? If at school, how were your students affected?

Thomas Edison, one of the greatest inventors in history, secured over one thousand different patents. Like Jordan, Edison recognized that the path to success is messy, and failing forward is a part of the journey. It's been said that it took Edison over ten thousand attempts to create the first commercial incandescent light bulb. It's also been said that Edison's mindset wasn't that he failed ten thousand times but that he believed he found ten thousand ways that didn't work.

Failing forward isn't merely a mindset. It's also about learning how to persevere through adversity.

R. H. Macy failed in retail seven times before his store in New York City finally stayed open. Beethoven's teacher called him "hopeless" and said he didn't have a future as a composer. Hank Aaron started his major league career going zero for five in a nine-to-eight Braves loss to Cincinnati. Vera Wang failed to make the 1968 U.S. Olympic figure skating team, so she took a job as an assistant at *Vogue*, where she was promoted to senior fashion editor within a year at the age of twenty-three. Ten years later, she was passed over as the magazine's editor-in-chief, yet I'm sure you've heard of the world-famous brand that now goes by her name. J.K. Rowling had a book idea about a boy wizard that twelve publishers turned down. In high school, the late Robin Williams's classmates voted him "Least Likely to Succeed" after graduation. Three months after signing her first record deal, Lady Gaga's contract was canceled after producer L.A. Reid played her music in a meeting.

FAILING FORWARD ISN'T MERELY A MINDSET. IT'S ALSO ABOUT LEARNING HOW TO PERSEVERE THROUGH ADVERSITY.

Stop & REFLECT

Besides the well-known examples shared above, who inspires you to fail forward? Who needs that same inspiration from you?

Our world is filled with excuses. Do you have one as well? The road to success can be brutal. It is bumpy with many twists and turns. The road to success is also often unseen. But the journey, when we remain focused on the kids we serve, is always worth it.

Coming into the 2017–2018 season, the Philadelphia Eagles had never won a Super Bowl title, and their hopes were riding on a young quarterback, Carson Wentz. With the playoffs on the horizon and the hopes of the fans high, Wentz went down with a season-ending ACL injury in the final weeks of the season. Few expected Nick Foles, a quarterback who had almost retired at twenty-six years old after having been released by two other teams, to be able to lead the team much further.

With the regular season over, yet having a good enough record to make the playoffs, Foles didn't give up on his dreams. Foles rose to the challenge and led what would later be recognized as one of the most spectacular postseasons in NFL history. In the NFC Championship game, with the winner advancing to the Super Bowl, Foles faced his toughest challenge to date, the NFL's top-rated defense, the Minnesota Vikings.

Completing twenty-eight of thirty-four passes for 373 yards and three touchdowns, as well as running for another, Foles wrote himself into the NFL history books with one of the greatest performances of his career while leading his team to the Super Bowl.

In leading the Eagles to Super Bowl LII, the NFC champion Philadelphia Eagles faced the AFC and defending Super Bowl Champion New England Patriots, led by their legendary coach, Bill Belichick. With two minutes and twenty-one seconds remaining in the final quarter of play, Foles threw the go-ahead touchdown, and the Eagles went on to win their first Super Bowl in franchise history in a forty-one to thirty-three victory. After the game, Nick Foles, a player who other teams had previously decided was no longer worth a roster spot, was named the Most Valuable Player of Super Bowl LII.

The day following the greatest accomplishment of his football career, Foles was asked to reflect on his journey and his future playing in Philadelphia, with Wentz returning as the starting quarterback the following year. It would have been easy for Foles to have a prideful mindset. It would have been easy for Foles to blast those teams who had cut him from their roster and didn't believe in him. Yet here's how he responded:

"I think the big thing is don't be afraid to fail. I think in our society today, with Instagram and Twitter, it's a highlight real. It's all the good things. When you look at it, you know, you think, wow, when you have a rough day, or you think your life is not as good as that, you're failing. Failure is a part of life. It's a part of building character and growing. Without failure, who would you be? I wouldn't be up here if I hadn't fallen thousands of times, made mistakes. We all are human. We all have weaknesses. I think through-out this, just being able to share that and be transparent. I know when I listen to people speak and share their weaknesses, I'm listening. Because I can resonate [relate]. So I'm not perfect. I'm not Superman. We might be in the NFL and we might have just won the Super Bowl, but we still have daily struggles. I still have daily struggles. That's where my faith comes in. That's where my family comes in. I think when you look at a struggle in your life, just know that it's an opportunity for your character to grow."[3]

Humility, when combined with perseverance and resilience and driven by a fail-forward mindset, offers those doing the work a winning formula for success.

Although he may suit up to take the field every day and not stand before kids in a classroom, Foles' fail-forward mindset, intertwined with persever-ance and resilience during the difficult times, and humility in the best of times, make those around him want to follow. His leadership makes those around him want to be on his team and perform well. His actions help to define the winning culture of his team.

It is *your* leadership, *your* perseverance, *your* resilience, and *your* fail-forward mindset that will ultimately define your success, whether in the classroom or running a school building. It is your mindset and actions that will have an impact on those you're in the trenches with each day.

Moments of uncertainty create opportunities for your leadership leg-acy. Failing forward with perseverance disciplines our own expectations, pushes us to keep trying, and ultimately empowers us to lead from within.

It is your display of humility in the best of times and your fail-forward mind-set and perseverance during the difficult times that will make those around you want to follow.

Stop & REFLECT

How do you model this type of mindset to those around you?

In my opinion, the educators who make the largest impact talk about and focus on opportunities. Less effective educators talk about and focus on obstacles. The difference is found in the lens in which one views the world: one's mindset. By choosing our lens, we allow ourselves to not only see our successes but also see opportunities instead of failures. There is so much power in the lens we choose.

As a teacher, how do you model this in your classroom? What's something that you want to try but have hesitated to do so? As an administrator, how do you model this mindset to those you lead? What's something you have wanted to lead but have been hesitant to initiate?

Every time we fail is an opportunity to model how to get up and keep trying to those who look to us for direction.

Superintendents: Failing forward through perseverance, resilience, and humility is a model showing your administrative team and teachers how to do so.

Principals: Failing forward through perseverance, resilience, and humility is a model showing your teachers and support staff how to do so.

Teachers: Failing forward through perseverance, resilience, and humility is a model showing your students how to do so.

EVERY TIME WE FAIL IS AN OPPORTUNITY TO MODEL HOW TO GET UP AND KEEP TRYING TO THOSE WHO LOOK TO US FOR DIRECTION.

Perseverance, resilience, and a fail-forward mindset are not standards that you'll see on any state assessment. They are far more important than that. They are *personal* and *authentic* life skills. In life, we become who we are, in part, because of the struggles we overcome. We become who we are by failing forward and persevering through adversity.

Life is determined not by the things that we want but by the choices that we make along the way. Regardless of our role on the team, we must internalize and own the impact of our actions. Failing forward, through perseverance and resilience when combined with humility, provides an amazing accelerator on the *personal* and *authentic* journey.

LIFE IS DETERMINED NOT BY THE THINGS THAT WE WANT BUT BY THE CHOICES THAT WE MAKE ALONG THE WAY.

Stop & REFLECT

> Teachers: Which student in your classroom is discouraged and needs additional support to fail forward? How will you support him or her?

> Administrators: Which person on your staff is discouraged and needs additional support to fail forward? How will you support him or her?

Try This

> Have the courage to be vulnerable. Those around you can't relate to someone they think is a perfect person. Be transparent in your failures and use your stories of failing forward to encourage those around you.

> Acknowledge students and staff that persevere through adversity. Let them know they are an inspiration and thank them for modeling how to handle difficult situations.

> During the best of times, lead with humility. During the difficult times, lead with humility.

> Celebrate those around you who fail forward and recognize their perseverance and resilience when highlighting their success.

> Display empathy for others—always. Know that struggles today build resilience for tomorrow.

EMPOWERING AGENCY WITH EMPATHY

"The illiterate of the twenty-first century will not be those who cannot read and write but those who cannot learn, unlearn, and relearn."

—ALVIN TOFFLER

Let's start this section off with a quick quiz. Without looking it up, what two colors are a stop sign and how many sides does it have?

I'm guessing that you considered it for a moment and thought red and white with eight sides. All right, let's try another question. What two colors are a yield sign and how many sides does it have?

If you're like many people, you know yield signs have three sides and are yellow and black. Right? In the United States, they were up until 1971, when they changed to the same two colors as the stop sign. Don't believe me? Look it up! Why is it that when asked, so many people still respond that they are yellow and black with three sides decades later?

It's common for human beings to learn something or naturally associate something in our minds with something else (like a yellow traffic light). The reality is that it's often difficult to *unlearn* and then *relearn* something.

The ability for students (and adults) to learn, unlearn, and relearn is at the core of learner agency, which is the ultimate goal of *personal* and *authentic* learning. Whether it's the state of society or the world of work, the only thing that remains constant is change. It's a paradox. It's also precisely why we must leverage *personal* and *authentic* learning experiences to help mold learners who can think independently, problem-solve, obtain the needed resources, act, and ultimately own the outcomes of their decisions. Learners with agency will solve the problems that our generations never could. Learners with agency will create the next iteration of jobs to replace those that have been automated. Learners with agency will succeed far past any graduation date.

Stop & REFLECT

What's something that you've recently had to unlearn and then relearn? What emotions did you feel in that process? What type of growth occurred?

The notion of "learner agency" is complex and interwoven with our own biases and beliefs as to what we believe kids are capable of in our classrooms and schools. Promoting learner agency also simultaneously abdicates some control to someone other than the teacher, a concept that is difficult for many. The traditional structure of school and its factors of influence have often limited the capacity of such agency, as following a prescribed path with most aspects "delivered to" the learner have minimized ownership in the learning process.

To be clear, learner agency is not about learners doing whatever they want when they want. It's not a designed free-for-all. Learner agency is also not about giving up the learning community to work independently and in isolation for long periods of time. Learner agency is about providing the learner with meaningful choices and promoting opportunities to exercise that decision-making while developing capacity and ownership over the learning and subsequent outcomes.

LEARNER AGENCY IS ABOUT PROVIDING THE LEARNER WITH MEANINGFUL CHOICES AND PROMOTING OPPORTUNITIES TO EXERCISE THAT DECISION-MAKING WHILE DEVELOPING CAPACITY AND OWNERSHIP OVER THE LEARNING AND SUBSEQUENT OUTCOMES.

The ability to build agency evolves alongside the maturity levels found inside each learner. It's essential to understand that the development of learner agency is not linear but grows as the learner becomes more responsible and self-reliant; thus, we must recognize that each child's level of agency will be unique. As such, the only way to maximize learner agency is through learning that is *personal* and *authentic*.

According to Education Reimagined,[4] learner agency can be visible in the following ways:

1. Learners develop a sense of ownership regarding their own learning, including a passion for learning, an ability to both create their learning experiences and assess the outcomes, and an interest in continually improving their learning experiences.

2. Learners develop the capacity to articulate their own learning needs and desires with insight into how they learn best and

what they specifically need to support their own learning and development.

3. Learners develop adaptability, resourcefulness, and resilience as they handle increasing responsibility for their own learning, informed equally by successful and failed learning experiments.
4. Learners develop a growing self-assuredness and self-confidence with regard to their capacity to direct their own learning, create their own learning experiences, and engage in unstructured learning challenges.
5. Learners experience themselves and their ideas as valued and as valuable; they develop an associated sense of self-worth.
6. Learners, having been supported in taking full ownership of their learning, leave organized education ready to be lifelong learners.

Where do *personal* and *authentic* learning experiences exist in your classroom or school to promote the type of agency our learners need to thrive well into their futures?

Stop & REFLECT

Every educator works to help students own their learning. How do you model that to students in your role?

Agency thrives when students understand themselves as learners, understand how to advocate and seek out what it is they need, and ultimately develop confidence in their own executive function and self-regulation. As learners mature in understanding that they are, in fact, learners, we must also help them understand the need for empathy for others.

Merriam-Webster defines empathy as "the action of understanding, being aware of, being sensitive to, and vicariously experiencing the feelings, thoughts, and experience of another of either the past or present without having the feelings, thoughts, and experience fully communicated in an objectively explicit manner."[5]

Agency, when paired with empathy, empowers an independent person who also cares about and wants to help others, skills desperately needed in the world around us.

One example of learner agency is a child's ability to independently research, curate, and develop an understanding regarding homelessness in the community and then present their findings. When paired with empathy, the learner then feels compelled to actually do something to help the situation.

Today's learners need to develop the agency to be independent and successfully solve the problems that come their way while also having the empathy to see the world through the eyes of others. Understanding the stories of others and having the ability to act on them in a supportive way builds the type of individuals our world so desperately needs.

UNDERSTANDING THE STORIES OF OTHERS AND HAVING THE ABILITY TO ACT ON THEM IN A SUPPORTIVE WAY BUILDS THE TYPE OF INDIVIDUALS OUR WORLD SO DESPERATELY NEEDS.

Stop & REFLECT

How can you help students develop both agency and empathy? How do you model empathy in your daily interactions with those around you?

Try This

> Have students research current issues in their community. As a class, develop a game plan to tackle one of the issues, even just a little bit.

> Study diverse individuals throughout history who overcame obstacles and were able to make an impact or leave their marks due to agency and perseverance. Discuss empathy for the individual throughout the process.

> Prior to graduation, engage students in a tradition called "Senior Talks." These talks celebrate the diverse achievements and experiences of each individual, as the soon-to-be graduates reflect on their personal growth, which is then, in turn, celebrated by the learning community.

> Develop meaningful, ongoing relationships with senior centers
and places that support adults with special needs. Have
students connect with these adults in a variety of ways, including
written school concert invitations, pen pal letters, and picnics.

FROM HEARTACHE TO HOPE

"Learn from yesterday, live for today, hope for tomorrow."
—ALBERT EINSTEIN

January 6, 2017, began like so many other travel days for me. After speaking
at an event the night before, I woke up, packed my belongings at the hotel,
grabbed breakfast with some people I had met, and caught an Uber ride to
the Fort Lauderdale airport. Little did I know how much I'd learn that day
about what it really means to be *personal* and *authentic*—as educators and
in life itself.

After traveling to the airport with a group of three others from the event,
we worked our way through security, grabbed some coffee, and discussed
our trips home for a few moments. A few handshakes later, I was off to my
gate in Terminal 2, as my flight was one of the first ones to depart, and I
was set to travel back home to Philadelphia after a brief layover in Atlanta.
I boarded the plane like I'd done hundreds of times before, checked in on
social media from the airport, and it was wheels up soon thereafter.

As my plane descended into Atlanta about ninety minutes later, after
turning my phone back on, it began to vibrate nonstop, to the point that
I thought someone was calling me the moment I had gained reception. I
pulled my phone out of my pocket and saw that it wasn't ringing but that
text messages were coming through—twenty-seven of them to be exact.

"Are you still there?"

"Are you okay? Please respond."

My heart stopped. It was apparent something had happened during my
short flight from Fort Lauderdale to Atlanta. I quickly began searching on
my phone and the breaking news sent chills down my spine.

*I'm at the Ft. Lauderdale Airport. Shots have been fired. Everyone is run-
ning. —@AriFleischer[6]*

*There is an ongoing incident in Terminal 2, baggage claim. Media avail-
ability is at the staging area. —Fort Lauderdale-Hollywood Int'l Airport
(FLL), @FLLFlyer[7]*

As we landed, word on our plane started to spread about the shooting that had just occurred in Terminal 2, the same Delta terminal from which we had just departed. Although I was never remotely in harm's way, I will admit that I was shaken to my core.

Walking to my gate, I responded to the messages, starting first with my family members who were texting and calling. As I approached the gate for my next flight, I noticed the heavy police presence that was developing in the terminal. I stood there quietly reflecting, shaken on the inside. It's hard to describe what went through my mind during those brief moments.

A few minutes later, the thoughts that ran through my mind were disrupted by an older gentleman's voice singing softly about ten feet behind me. His deep, southern, male voice and the gospel music he was singing were both calming and reassuring. When I turned around, I noticed that he was sitting there, ready to shine the shoes of any of the many travelers who crossed his path that day. When we exchanged glances, he gave me a bright, warm smile and asked, "Can I help you today?"

"You already have, sir," I responded.

I can tell you that traveling every week, I've walked past hundreds of places where I could have had my shoes shined. I've never really given it any thought to do so. Yet that morning, I figured it'd be worth the eight dollars posted on this man's sign, walked toward him, and told him that it'd be an honor to spend some time with him. For me, it was about far more than needing my shoes cleaned early that afternoon. This man radiated hope, and with the thoughts that raced through my mind, I knew I could sure use it.

The man with the warm smile and a great gospel voice gave me a firm handshake, grabbed my luggage, wiped off my seat, and began to do his thing. I'll admit that the thought of paying someone else to shine my shoes as I traveled seemed a bit awkward. But for me, at that moment, his song and warm smile were precisely what I needed. I felt compelled to talk to this man, as his songs had pulled me away from the sad and emotional thoughts I was having only a few moments prior.

The ten minutes I spent with Gus, a wonderful man from Georgia who shines shoes for a living, were ten minutes I'll never forget. They were also ten minutes that taught me so much about what being *personal* and *authentic* really means.

Gus began by taking a good look at my shoes from top to bottom, front to back. As only he could, he let out a small chuckle and said, "Boy, your shoes need some work! Let me take good care of you." Needing the laugh, I let Gus know how much I appreciated him and thanked him for being so kind and helpful. I then asked Gus how long he had been shining shoes.

"Twenty-six great years!" he responded.

Knowing I could learn something from this wise man, I smiled and said, "Wow, I'm honored to have such an experienced veteran helping me. Tell me, Gus, what's made the years so great?"

Gus looked me right in the eye, smiled, and said, "Son, life is short. You've got to have fun and love life every day. I love the work that I get to do. I could have retired years ago, but I love helping people and don't want to stop."

I'll humbly admit, through my own biased lens, when I woke up that morning, I certainly would not have put shining shoes at an airport on the top of my career bucket list. Yet Gus did just that, and in the next few moments, I'd begin to see how this fine man was following his passion for helping people and how he was *personal* and *authentic* every day.

For the next ten minutes, Gus communicated exactly what he was doing, why he was using the different cleaners, why he was using certain polishes, and how it would definitely help me "look sharp" for my trip back home to my family. For those ten minutes, I watched this older man, probably in his late seventies, take enormous pride in his work. I could tell Gus was doing everything he could, even down to the detailed work with a cotton swab, to ensure that every inch of my previously beat-up shoes looked brand new. For those ten minutes, I felt like the most important customer in the world. Gus literally wanted me to shine.

Before finishing the job, Gus looked at his work from different angles, both up close and from a few feet away, and when he was personally satisfied, he looked at me and said, "So, Tom, I think you look sharp and are ready to go get on that airplane. What do you think? Are you happy with it, or is there something I can do to make it better?"

I'll admit, I sat there in awe. Those ten minutes with Gus caused me to reflect not just on education but on life itself. I pulled out my wallet and didn't want to pay him the eight dollars plus the tip he was owed. I felt so compelled to give him all that I had. He had taken such great care of me at a time when I was an emotional mess, and the very least I could do was take great care of him in return.

"Gus, my friend, you are an amazing man, and as the dad of two young kids, I hope someday they turn out to be just like you. Thank you for making my day and for the privilege of having you give me the world's best shoe shine. Now take your beautiful wife that you were telling me about out on a date—on me. Gus, you did far more than you realize. Thank you, my friend."

Stop & REFLECT

Do you know a *personal* and *authentic* person like Gus? What lessons does that person model of how to be an incredible educator?

With that, I boarded the flight to Philadelphia and began to write down a few notes, things I learned from the incredible man who had single-handedly altered my mindset. These "Lessons from Gus" give incredible insight into what being *personal* and *authentic* as educators is all about.

1. GUS ALTERED THE MINDSET AND MADE THE DAY OF A COMPLETE STRANGER.

His radiance of hope drew me toward him at a time when I really needed it. In a few short minutes, Gus brought me from heartache to hope, without ever realizing what I had on my heart the moment he asked if he could help.

Personal & Authentic Lesson: Our interactions with those we serve can be life-changing, and we may never understand the full extent. You'll never know the battles that others may be facing at the very moment you have the chance to help them. Every child that walks through our school doors is an opportunity. Make every interaction count.

2. GUS LOVED HIS WORK, AND HIS PASSION FOR IT RADIATED.

For every second of our interaction, it was obvious that Gus loved what he did. It was clear that he aimed to be the very best at his craft. He took immense pride in his work and led with a servant's heart.

Personal & Authentic Lesson: As educators, we must lead with passion and never settle for anything less than our very best. Let the love of your work so radiate that it inspires others to give their best. Be proud of what you do and the impact that you have!

3. GUS TOOK OWNERSHIP OF HIS WORK AND HIS ATTENTION TO DETAIL WAS IMPECCABLE.

Gus wanted things to be perfect for those he served and for his work to exceed their expectations. He exemplified a true customer service mindset.

The attention to detail that Gus gave me led me to believe he was the very best in the world at what he did.

Personal & Authentic Lesson: Own your actions and know they speak more than your words ever will. Do everything to the very best of your ability, as trivial as a task may seem, and give it your all. It may be your only, or last, opportunity to do so. Our work as educators is far too important not to give it our very best.

4. GUS'S HAPPINESS CAME FROM SERVING OTHERS, LOVING HIS FAMILY, AND HIS MINDSET.

Although I could be wrong, I'm guessing as a professional shoe shiner, Gus isn't very wealthy by the world's definition. But his priorities and mindset, in my opinion, made him one of the wealthiest people I've ever met.

Personal & Authentic Lesson: Your mindset matters. Surround yourself with positive people who have a can-do mentality and will lovingly push you to be better. Know that true happiness does not come from material things but from your family, your relationships, and through serving others well.

5. GUS MADE ME FEEL LIKE THE MOST IMPORTANT CUSTOMER IN THE WORLD EVERY MOMENT WE WERE TOGETHER.

In a world filled with every possible distraction and directly in the midst of the chaos of one of the busiest airports in the world, Gus made me feel like I was the only one that mattered when I was with him. He wasn't distracted on his cell phone, looking at all those who passed, or talking to his nearby coworker. He was focused on me and completely present with the person he was eager to serve.

Personal & Authentic Lesson: Be present. Every waking moment is a chance to build a relationship with someone, somewhere, and to show another person, even one you may not know, that they matter. Remain focused on who we serve and why we do the work that we do.

As I drove home a few hours later, I kept the radio off as I reflected on the tragic events of that morning in Fort Lauderdale, prayed for my friends who remained locked down at the airport, and finally, on my ten-minute interaction with Gus—a man whose mindset and life experience taught me far more about being *personal* and *authentic* than I could repay that afternoon during a layover in Atlanta.

Later that day, Paisley came running in from school, excited about her day and anxious to share all that had happened. Her innocence and love for others radiated. I hugged her tight and tried not to allow her to see my tears. I knew that someday her little world would be exposed to the kind of evil that occurred that morning, the type of evil that took the lives of Mary Louise Amzibel, Terry Andres, Michael Oehme, Shirley Timmons, and Olga Woltering only a few hours earlier, innocent people who had stories and whose lives mattered. As I held her tight, I mourned their loss and felt a deep sadness. Yet during those moments, I also felt an incredible sense of hope.

As I stood in the middle of my kitchen with my arms around my little girl, I felt that sense of hope because of people like Gus.

Because of people like you.

Your legacy will not be determined by the content you taught but by how well you served others. It is educators who walk the walk, just like Gus, who make the largest impact and whose fingerprints will be visible on the lives of others for generations to come as they leave the greatest legacies.

YOUR LEGACY WILL NOT BE DETERMINED BY THE CONTENT YOU TAUGHT BUT BY HOW WELL YOU SERVED OTHERS.

Stop & REFLECT

What is it that gives you hope as an educator? What hope do you have in your students and those who serve kids alongside you each day? Do they know you feel that way?

Try This

> Take some time to reflect on the legacy you believe you've already built. Write a letter to yourself about the things you want people to say about you once you're no longer in your current role. Keep that paper in the front of your plan book or in a folder in your desk. Reflect on it as often as necessary.

> At the end of a school year, choose someone who is retiring and write them a letter about the legacy they will leave and what you respect most about them.

> Design a legacy activity with students and have them create something (e.g., letter, time capsule, etc.) that will be opened during their senior graduation week that reflects on the legacy that they hope to leave while in school.

MAKING IT HAPPEN

"The ones who are crazy enough to think that they can change the world are the ones that do."

—STEVE JOBS

The choice is yours.

The legacy that you build and will leave behind someday is something you must own. So teach and lead with no regrets. Your impact can never, and will never, be erased. Your work matters, and it matters every single day.

Don't lose sight that the main purpose of *personal* and *authentic* learning isn't about getting kids ready for college or careers. *Personal* and *authentic* learning is about helping kids become ready for life and, ultimately, successful at whatever they choose to do.

The number of educators who want to change, but are paralyzed by what others might think or say, equals the number of educators who are losing precious time to increase their level of impact. Don't allow self-doubt or the fear of what others may think steal the joy felt in the payoff of moving your work for kids forward. Insecurity is a seed that germinates, and if you continue to feed the soil around it, it'll grow roots and create cracks in your foundation. Don't allow the poison of that insecurity to become you. The work you do every day is far too important. Our kids are far too important.

On your *personal* and *authentic* journey, surround yourself with people who will walk with you as you move forward. Many of the things you're yearning for today are just past the fear exit on your own highway to success. You can't improve what you avoid so gather with those who will help you navigate the journey and hold you accountable along the way.

EVERY CHILD IN OUR CLASSROOMS AND IN OUR SCHOOLS IS SOMEONE ELSE'S WHOLE WORLD.

Remain focused on your why to ensure that you don't lose your way. Fail early, fail often, and never stop learning. Failing sooner often enables us to succeed faster. Be proud of your work and always lead with humility. Our kids desperately need *personal* and *authentic* role models. They need you.

Every child in our classrooms and in our schools is someone else's whole world. Do we teach like that? Do we lead like that? Do we love them like that?

Every day is an opportunity to maximize your impact if you choose to see it that way. Your choices today will build your legacy for tomorrow. Years from now, many will reflect on that legacy. The good news is that you get to choose how you will be remembered. The choices that go into this are made and lived out every single day.

Make their experience *personal* and *authentic*.

Make the culture around you *personal* and *authentic*.

Make your relationships *personal* and *authentic*.

Be *personal* and *authentic* . . .

. . . and your fingerprints will be on the lives of so many for generations to come.

The work is hard, but our kids are worth it.

Be bold. Be fearless. Be proud. Be you.

Your story is not finished yet.

All for the kids we serve,

A CLOSER LOOK

For a deeper dive into Chapter 7 as well as free tools, resources, and study guide questions, visit **thomascmurray.com/AuthenticEDU7**.

BIBLIOGRAPHY

CHAPTER 1

1. Shallwani, P. "Couple from Macungie killed in fiery accident on Turnpike." *The Morning Call* (Allentown, PA), April 12, 2001.

CHAPTER 2

1. Sheninger, Eric C. and Thomas C. Murray. *Learning Transformed: 8 Keys to Designing Tomorrow's Schools, Today.* Alexandria, VA: ASCD, 2017.
2. Cook, C., Fiat, A., and M. Larson. "Positive Greetings at the Door: Evaluation of a Low-Cost, High-Yield Proactive Classroom Management Strategy." *Journal of Positive Behavior Interventions* 20, no. 3 (2018): 149-159. journals.sagepub.com/doi/10.1177/1098300717753831.
3. Cook, C., et al. "Positive Greetings at the Door: Evaluation of a Low-Cost, High-Yield Proactive Classroom Management Strategy.". February 19, 2018. https://doi.org/10.1177/1098300717753831.
4. Kroll, L., and K. Dolan. "Billionaires: The Richest People in the World." Forbes.com, March 5, 2019. forbes.com/billionaires/#46be5868251c.
5. "Oprah Winfrey Biography." *Encyclopedia of World Biography.* (n.d.). Retrieved August 4, 2019. notablebiographies.com/We-Z/Winfrey-Oprah.html.

CHAPTER 3

1. Sinek, Simon. "Start with Why: How Great Leaders Inspire Action." TEDxPugent Sound. September 2009. ted.com/talks/simon_sinek_how_great_leaders_inspire_action.
2. FranklinCovey. "The Hidden Story." Kaleidoscope Films. Adforum Video, 2:55. bit.ly/TheHiddenStories.

CHAPTER 4

1. Ramsey, Dave. "Shooting the Sacred Cows." *DaveRamsey.com* (blog). Accessed August 1, 2019. daveramsey.com/blog/shooting-the-sacred-cows.
2. Frost, Robert. "Title." In *The New Speaker's Treasury of Wit and Wisdom*, edited by Herbert Victor Prochnow. New York: Harper Collins, 1958.
3. Gallman, Stephanie. "Elite runner crawls across the finish line at Austin Marathon." *CNN.com*. February 17, 2015. cnn.com/2015/02/16/us/austin-marathon-finish-line-crawl.
4. "Introduction to the Learning Sciences." *Digital Promise: Accelerating Innovation in Education*. 2018. researchmap.digitalpromise.org/topics/introduction-learning-sciences.
5. "Introduction to the Learning Sciences." *Digital Promise*.

CHAPTER 5

1. Horowitz, J., and N. Graf. "Most U.S. Teens See Anxiety and Depression as a Major Problem Among Their Peers." *Pew Research Center*. February 20, 2019. pewsocialtrends.org/2019/02/20/most-u-s-teens-see-anxiety-and-depression-as-a-major-problem-among-their-peers.
2. Maslow, A.H. "A Theory of Human Motivation." *Psychological Review* 50 (1943): 370-396.
3. Maslow, Abraham. "Hierarchy of Needs." *Creative Commons*. commons.wikimedia.org/wiki/File:Maslow%27s_Hierarchy_of_Needs.svg
4. Korbey, Holly. "The Power of Being Seen." *Edutopia*. October 27, 2017. edutopia.org/article/power-being-seen.
5. "Mental Health by the Numbers." *National Alliance on Mental Illness (nami.org)*. nami.org/learn-more/mental-health-by-the-numbers.
6. "Suicide Among Youth." Center for Disease Control and Prevention. September 15, 2017). cdc.gov/healthcommunication/toolstemplates/entertainmented/tips/suicideyouth.html.
7. "From a Nation at Risk to a Nation at Hope." *National Commission on Social, Emotional, and Academic Development*. (2019). The Aspen Institute. nationathope.org/wp-content/uploads/2018_aspen_final-report_full_webversion.pdf.

8. Fry, R. and Parker, K. "Early Benchmarks Show 'Post-Millennials' on Track to Be Most Diverse, Best-Educated Generation Yet." *Pew Research Center*. November 5, 2018. pewsocialtrends.org/2018/11/15/early-benchmarks-show-post-millennials-on-track-to-be-most-diverse-best-educated-generation-yet.

9. Fry, R. "Early Benchmarks."

10. Irvine, Jacqueline, and Hawley, W. "Culturally Responsive Pedagogy: An Overview of Research on Student Outcomes." *EdWeek*. edweek.org/media/crt_research.pdf.

11. Piff, P., I. Dietze, et al. "Awe, the Small Self, and Prosocial Behavior." *American Psychological Association, Journal of Personality and Social Psychology*, 108 # 6, (2015): 883–899. apa.org/pubs/journals/releases/psp-pspi0000018.pdf.

12. Silva, Jason. (2013). "Shots of Awe." *TestTube*. youtube.com/watch?v=8QyVZrV3d3o.

13. O'Kane, Caitlin. "High School robotics team builds electric wheelchair for 2-year-old whose family couldn't afford one." *CBS News*, April 2, 2011.

14. Beckman, Brittany L. "The DIY Girls: How 12 teens invented a solar-powered tent for the homeless." *Mashable*. June 15, 2017. mashable.com/2017/06/15/diy-girls-solar-powered-tent-homeless.

15. Spencer, John. "Why Consuming Is Necessary for Creating." *The Creative Classroom*. February 25, 2019. youtube.com/watch?v=MDXyr2YSxbA.

16. Spencer, J. "Why Consuming Is Necessary."

17. Sparks, Sarah. "Getting Feedback Right: A Q&A With John Hattie." *Education Week*. June 19, 2018. edweek.org/ew/articles/2018/06/20/getting-feedback-right-a-qa-with-john.html.

OTHER NOTES:

GoBabyGo: sites.udel.edu/gobabygo

CHAPTER 6

1. Prosthetic Kids Hand Challenge. (n.d.). "The kids and Teacher Behind the Challenge: Our Story." handchallenge.com/about-us.html.

2. Dunlap, Tiare. "Sixth Graders Make 3D Printed Prosthetic Hands for Kids in Need." *People.com*. June 1, 2015. people.com/human-interest/sixth-graders-3d-print-prosthetic-hands-for-kids.

3. Darling-Hammond, L., M. Zielezinski, and S. Goldman. "Using technology to support at-risk students' learning." Stanford, CA: The Alliance for Excellent Education and Stanford Center for Opportunity Policy in Education, 2014.
4. Funk, C., and Parker, K. "Blacks in STEM jobs are especially concerned about diversity and discrimination in the workplace." *Pew Research Center.* January 9, 2018. pewsocialtrends.org/2018/01/09/blacks-in-stem-jobs-are-especially-concerned-about-diversity-and-discrimination-in-the-workplace.
5. Horrigan, J. "The numbers behind the broadband 'homework gap.'" *Pew Research Center*, 2015. pewresearch.org/fact-tank/2015/04/20/the-numbers-behindthe-broadband-homework-gap.
6. Barrett, P., Zhang, Y., Davies, F., and Barrett, L. (February 2015). "Clever Classrooms: Summary Report of the HEAD Project (Holistic Evidence and Design)." *University of Salford Manchester.* salford.ac.uk/cleverclassrooms/1503-Salford-Uni-Report-DIGITAL.pdf.
7. Thornburg, D. (2007). Campfires in Cyberspace: Primordial Metaphors for learning in the 21st Century. Thornburg Center for Professional Development. p. 1-12.

IMAGE CREDIT:

Craft, Chris (@crafty184). "@americanair This sweet boy had his first plane trip today, raising awareness about limb differences. Check out that 3D-printed prosthetic." December 13, 2016, 5:12 PM. Tweet. twitter.com/crafty184/status/808796844021190656.

CHAPTER 7

1. Lipman, V. "Ever Feel Career Odds Are Stacked Against You? Try Reading Tom Brady's Old NFL Scouting Report." *Forbes*, December 10, 2018. forbes.com/sites/victorlipman/2018/12/10/ever-feel-career-odds-are-stacked-against-you-try-reading-tom-bradys-old-nfl-scouting-report/#59d1b253217a.
2. Zorn, Eric. "Without Failure, Jordan Would be False Idol." *Chicago Tribune.* May 19, 1997. chicagotribune.com/news/ct-xpm-1997-05-19-9705190096-story.html.

3. Joseph, A. "Foles delivers heartfelt reflection about failure." *USA Today*. February 5, 2018. usatoday.com/story/sports/ftw/2018/02/05/nick-foles-delivers-heartfelt-reflection-about-failure-the-day-after-his-super-bowl-win/110140832.

4. "Practitioner's Lexicon: What is meant by key terminology." *Education Reimagined*. January 2018. education-reimagined.org/wp-content/uploads/2019/01/Revised-Lexicon_EDRE.pdf.

5. "Empathy." *Merriam-Webster*. merriam-webster.com/dictionary/empathy.

6. Fleischer, Ari (@AriFleischer). "I'm at the Ft. Lauderdale Airport. Shots have been fired. Everyone is running." January 6, 2017, 12:57 PM. twitter.com/AriFleischer/status/817429795113996288.

7. Fort Lauderdale-Hollywood Int'l Airport (FLL). (@FLLFlyer). *"There is an ongoing incident in Terminal 2, Baggage Claim. Media availability is at the staging area."* January 6, 2017, 1:16 PM. twitter.com/FLLFlyer/status/817434597919195137.

#AuthenticEDU

ACKNOWLEDGMENTS

Thank you to my good friend, Inky Johson, for writing the foreword to this book. Your story of courage and resilience has motivated so many, including me. A special thank you to Dr. Rosa Perez-Isiah and Ken Shelton for coauthoring portions of this book and for all of the incredible support along the way. Also, thank you to Matt Miller, Dr. Justin Aglio, Michael McCormick, Dr. Adam Phyall, and Uma Purani for sharing a part of their stories alongside mine. Additionally, a special thank you to Trevor Guthke for creating many of the images as well as to the more than forty educators who freely shared their ideas and words of inspiration throughout these pages.

BRING THOMAS C. MURRAY TO YOUR SCHOOL OR EVENT

Thomas C. Murray offers inspirational and engaging keynotes, workshops, and customized professional learning programs. His motivating blend of personal stories, evidence-based practices, and practical ideas for implementing *personal* and *authentic* learning is experienced by tens of thousands of educators each year. Having served at the classroom, building, and district level, Murray works directly with audiences at all levels. Whether leading an administrative retreat, keynoting a conference for thousands of teachers, working alongside a region of superintendents, or helping to kick off a school year at opening convocation, Murray leads through humility while challenging educators to give their all for kids and take care of themselves along the way.

WHAT PEOPLE ARE SAYING ABOUT THOMAS C. MURRAY

"Talk about creating energy, excitement, and commanding the room. Two minutes in and I'm hooked. This guy is amazing. @thomascmurray #ISTE19"

— @KENNISDANI

"@thomascmurray made a huge impact on all teachers and admins today at @EastPennSD! One of the most humble, personal, appreciative, and down-to-earth keynotes I've ever heard. Thank you for being here! #EastPennProud"

— @DYLANDPETERSEDU

"Had the pleasure of opening our school year with @thomascmurray today. I've never been more moved or more motivated. Thank you, thank you, thank you."

— @LUCYANDLEIGH

"Thank you @thomascmurray for your time with @NYSchoolSupts today at #NYSuptsFall. You made us think, laugh & cry! #LeadersMatter"

— @CSDEDRICK

"#cvwelcomeback is blowing my mind! @thomascmurray is saying what we all need to hear. @CajonValleyUSD is revving up for an amazing year."

— @MISSKEFFER

"Looking for a 5-Star keynote? @thomascmurray is the real deal!! Brought it loud & clear today for @FredSchools. #Relationships"

— @JRUSSVT18

"@thomascmurray absolutely crushed MOASSP 2019 keynote. Second time seeing him in the last year. An hour and a half feels like 10 minutes when he speaks. Feeling inspired to lead. #MOSC2019"

— @DRLUHNINGVPHS

"Wow! Can Tom Murray be my hype man every year?!"

— @EVSKLEIN2

"@thomascmurray Chills. Tears. Starting the school year with a full heart."

— @MRSCOFFEECOOK

"If you don't cry, you actually are emotionless. This was incredible and a great reminder that we are all a family within the four walls of our schools. Thanks @thomascmurray for sharing this morning. #KansansCan"

— @RHUFFIC

POPULAR MESSAGES FROM THOMAS C. MURRAY

FOR THE ENTIRE DISTRICT

> Personal & Authentic: Designing Learning Experiences that Impact a Lifetime

> Learning Transformed: 8 Keys to Designing Tomorrow's Schools, Today

> From Research to Practice, Creating the Learning Spaces Kids Need

FOR ADMINISTRATORS

> Creating Future Ready Schools

> Leading with Purpose

> We Went 1:1, Now What?

FOR TEACHERS

> Tech Tools for Student Engagement and Teacher Effectiveness

> Digital Citizenship in Every Classroom

MORE FROM

IMPRESS

EMPOWER
What Happens When Student Own Their Learning
By A.J. Juliani and John Spencer

In an ever-changing world, educators and parents must take a role in helping students prepare themselves for *anything*. That means unleashing their creative potential! In *Empower*, **A.J. Juliani** and **John Spencer** provide teachers, coaches, and administrators with a roadmap that will inspire innovation, authentic learning experiences, and practical ways to empower students to pursue their passions while in school.

LEARNER–CENTERED INNOVATION
Spark Curiosity, Ignite Passion, and Unleash Genius
By Katie Martin

Learning opportunities and teaching methods *must* evolve to match the ever-changing needs of today's learners. In *Learner-Centered Innovation*, **Katie Martin** offers insights into how to make the necessary shifts and create an environment where learners at every level are empowered to take risks in pursuit of learning and growth rather than perfection.

UNLEASH TALENT
Bringing Out the Best in Yourself and the Learners You Serve
By Kara Knollmeyer

In *Unleash Talent*, educator and principal **Kara Knollmeyer** explains that by exploring the core elements of talent—passion, skills, and personality traits—you can uncover your gifts and help others do the same. Whether you are a teacher, administrator, or custodian, this insightful guide will empower you to use your unique talents to make a powerful impact on your school community.

RECLAIMING OUR CALLING
Hold on to the Heart, Mind, and Hope of Education
By Brad Gustafson

Children are more than numbers, and we are called to teach and reach them accordingly. In this genre-busting book, award-winning educator and principal **Brad Gustafson** uses stories to capture the heart, mind, and hope of education.

TAKE THE L.E.A.P
Ignite a Culture of Innovation
By Elisabeth Bostwick

Take the L.E.A.P.: Ignite a Culture of Innovation will inspire and support you as you to take steps to grow beyond traditional and self-imposed boundaries. Award-winning educator **Elisabeth Bostwick** shares stories and practical strategies to help you challenge conventional thinking and create the conditions that empower meaningful learning.

DRAWN TO TEACH
An Illustrated Guide to Transforming Your Teaching
Written by Josh Stumpenhorst, Illustrated by Trevor Guthke

If you're looking for ways to help your students succeed, you won't find the answer in gimmicks, trends, or fads. Great teaching isn't about test results or data; it's about connecting with students and empowering them to own their learning. Through this clever, illustrated guide, **Josh Stumpenhorst** reveals the key characteristics all top educators share in common and shows you how to implement them in your teaching practice.

MATH RECESS
Playful Learning in an Age of Disruption
By Sunil Singh and Dr. Christopher Brownell

In the theme of recess, where a treasure chest of balls, ropes, and toys would be kept for children to play with, this book holds a deep and imaginative collection of fun mathematical ideas, puzzles, and problems. Written for anyone interested in or actively engaged in schools—parents, teachers, administrators, school board members—this book shows math as a playful, fun, and wonderfully human activity that everyone can enjoy... for a lifetime!

INNOVATE INSIDE THE BOX
Empowering Learners Through UDL and Innovator's Mindset
By George Couros and Katie Novak

In *Innovate Inside the Box*, **George Couros** and **Katie Novak** provide informed insight on creating purposeful learning opportunities for all students. By combining the power of the Innovator's Mindset and Universal Design for Learning (UDL), they empower educators to create opportunities that will benefit every learner.

ABOUT THE AUTHOR

Thomas C. Murray serves as the director of innovation for Future Ready Schools®, a project of the Alliance for Excellent Education, located in Washington, D.C. He has testified before the United States Congress and has worked alongside that body and the U.S. Senate, the White House, the U.S. Department of Education and state departments of education and school districts throughout the country to implement *personal* and *authentic* learning. Murray serves regularly as a conference keynote speaker and was named the 2015 Education Policy Person of the Year by the Academy of Arts and Sciences, one of "20 to Watch in 2016" by the National School Boards Association, the 2017 Education Thought Leader of the Year by PR with Panache, and the National/Global EdTech Leader of the Year by EdTech Digest in 2018. He is often recognized as one of the top influencers in school leadership and educational technology. Prior to his current work, Murray spent fourteen years as a teacher, principal, and district level administrator in Bucks County, Pennsylvania. He currently lives in eastern Pennsylvania with his wife and two children.

Connect:

Web: thomascmurray.com
Twitter: @thomascmurray
YouTube: youtube.com/thomascmurray
Facebook: facebook.com/thomascmurrayEDU
Instagram: instagram.com/thomascmurrayEDU
Pinterest: pinterest.com/thomascmurray

CPSIA information can be obtained
at www.ICGtesting.com
Printed in the USA
BVHW040506240521
607685BV00001B/1

9 781948 334198